CUL

What are the qualities and properties that make something cultural? What does claiming something as cultural allow us to do?

*Culture* offers students a workable understanding of the category 'culture' and explores how the realm of the 'cultural' can be practically explored as a way of understanding the world.

Ben Highmore provides a clear and robust defence of the productivity of cultural analysis in a media-saturated world, while also instilling a sense of modesty in qualifying what can and can not be accomplished in the name of cultural analysis.

With extensive examples and case studies throughout, the book demonstrates both the productivity and the limitations in orientating analysis to the cultural.

A thought-provoking and engaging examination, *Culture* is an ideal introductory text for students of media and cultural studies.

**Ben Highmore** is Professor of Cultural Studies at the University of Sussex, UK. He is a key author in cultural studies and his research is broadly concerned with the culture of everyday life. His publications include *A Passion for Cultural Studies* (2009) and *Ordinary Lives: Studies in the Everyday* (2011).

# KEY IDEAS IN MEDIA AND CULTURAL STUDIES

The *Key Ideas in Media and Cultural Studies* series covers the main concepts, issues, debates and controversies in contemporary media and cultural studies. Titles in the series constitute authoritative, original essays rather than literary surveys, but are also written explicitly to support undergraduate teaching. The series provides students and teachers with lively and original treatments of key topics in the field.

*Cultural Policy* by David Bell and Kate Oakley
*Reality TV* by Annette Hill
*Culture* by Ben Highmore

Forthcoming:

*Representation* by Jenny Kidd
*Active Audiences* by Helen Wood
*Celebrity* by Sean Redmond
*Mediatization* by Andreas Hepp

# CULTURE

Ben Highmore

Routledge
Taylor & Francis Group

LONDON AND NEW YORK

First published 2016
by Routledge
2 Park Square, Milton Park, Abingdon, Oxon OX14 4RN

and by Routledge
711 Third Avenue, New York, NY 10017

*Routledge is an imprint of the Taylor & Francis Group, an informa business*

*British Library Cataloguing in Publication Data*
A catalogue record for this book is available from the British Library

*Library of Congress Cataloging in Publication Data*
Highmore, Ben, 1961-
Culture / by Ben Highmore. – 1 Edition.
pages cm. – (Key ideas in media and cultural studies)
Includes bibliographical references and index.
1. Culture. I. Title.
HM621.H4785 2015
306 – dc23
2015010184

ISBN: 978-0-415-67273-3 (hbk)
ISBN: 978-0-415-67274-0 (pbk)
ISBN: 978-0-203-12947-0 (ebk)

Typeset in Times New Roman by Taylor & Francis Books

MIX
Paper from
responsible sources
FSC
www.fsc.org   FSC® C013604

Printed and bound by CPI Group (UK) Ltd,
Croydon, CR0 4YY

# CONTENTS

List of figures                              vi
A note to the reader                         vii

1   **Introduction**                         1

2   **Landscape**                            23

3   **A whole way of life**                  46

4   **Politics**                             70

5   **Experience**                           95

6   **Death**                                117

7   **Two cheers for culture?**              138

Bibliography                                 159
Index                                        164

# LIST OF FIGURES

2.1 J. M. W. Turner, *The Fighting Téméraire, tugged to her last berth to be broken up,* 1839. Courtesy of The Art Archive/National Gallery London/Eileen Tweedy.    41

4.1 Edward Burtynsky, *Shipbreaking #27*, Chittagong, Bangladesh, 2000. © Edward Burtynsky, courtesy Nicholas Metivier Gallery, Toronto/Flowers, London.    84

4.2 Still from *Leviathan* (2012), directed by Lucien Castaing-Taylor and Verena Paravel.    87

4.3 Still from *The Forgotten Space* (2010), a film essay by Allan Sekula and Noël Burch.    89

4.4 Carole Condé and Karl Beveridge, *The Fall of Water*, 2007. © Carole Condé and Karl Beveridge, courtesy of the artists.    91

# A NOTE TO THE READER

The reason I'm writing this book is to try and clarify – for you *and* for me – what the term 'culture' refers to and how the realm of the cultural can be productively explored as a way of understanding the world. Two questions motivate this book. The first concerns the category of culture: what are we doing when we name something as culture or as cultural? What are we doing when we claim that some phenomenon belongs to the realm of the cultural? And the second question follows from this: what does claiming something as cultural allow us to do? What is the productivity of grasping something culturally? What forms of analysis does it encourage and discourage? What questions does it allow us to address and what questions become impossible or obscure? In other words if the first question asks what are the qualities and properties that make something cultural, the second question asks what sort of explanatory work does this then allow us to do.

In addressing these questions I also have to explain what culture *isn't* and what I think *isn't* a productive way of apprehending the world in the name of culture. But while I'm going to try and be as clear as possible I need to warn you right from the start that the road to clarity is not necessarily straight, and at times my task of clarification will also appear to complicate matters. I apologise for this, of course, but as the philosopher Jacques Derrida once put it, 'if things were simple, word would have gotten around' (Derrida 1988: 119). Academics, though, can over-complicate the world, going beyond what is necessarily complex and ending up with something altogether more obtuse and unwieldy. (Those amongst you who are academic sceptics might put this down to self-interest: after all if the world is made unfeasibly complicated then who else would have the time to study it apart from academics?) One way of holding back from an institutional tendency towards *unnecessary* over-complication is to take a pragmatist view and ask: what is the outcome of this or that complication? So the hope is that this is ultimately a practical book and one way of making it a practical book is for you, the reader, to test it out by putting it to work on your own examples.

In the 1980s and 1990s academics and intellectuals often signalled their dedication to complexity and difference by pluralising words like 'culture'. You could see the point when history showed you that 'culture' was often assumed to be the preserve of white middle-class men. So instead of American culture people would write about the 'cultures' of the United States. One unfortunate effect of this was that the plural of culture led to a myriad of isolated, singular 'cultures' – football culture, gay culture, women's culture, music culture and so on. I want to avoid this effect by assuming that culture is the word we give to the plurality and contradictions of meanings, feelings and practices that circulate in the world and, crucially, to their orchestration.

Lastly my choice of examples are not meant to suggest the full array of phenomena that would count as cultural. Perhaps all phenomena have a cultural aspect and a non-cultural aspect, certainly the examples I've become most attracted to in writing this book have. I have purposefully sought out phenomena that challenge some of the assumptions about what is most important about culture. Examples of illness and landscape, for instance, are useful for thinking about culture because there is, obviously, something about them that resists being subsumed and exhausted by cultural explanation. Whatever cultural accounts we might offer about this or that area of the planet's surface there are still rock formations, limestone, glacial movement, and so on. Whatever culture can tell us about the treatment and experience of illness there is still mortality, oxygen, neurons and blood – and let's face it, no one in their right mind wants to be confronted by an expert in matters of culture on the operating table.

While I was writing this book I was telling my fourteen-year-old son about it. I told him I was writing a whole book about one word. He said in a questioning way that I would also be writing about culture, not just about the word. I thought about it – it was true of course that I would necessarily be giving examples of culture, but this was intended to clarify the way the word circulated and the sorts of effects it had. His reply to this is probably as clear a description of the book as it would be possible to give: 'so you're writing about the culture of "culture"'.

# 1

# INTRODUCTION

In his book *Philosophical Investigations*, the philosopher Ludwig Wittgenstein stated that: 'for a *large* class of cases – though not for all – in which we employ the word "meaning" it can be defined thus: the meaning of a word is its use in the language' (1976 [1953]: 20, section 43). Wittgenstein's point is that if you want to understand a word – particularly a word that is used in everyday life rather than a word that has a specialised technical meaning (a medical term, for instance) – and you want to get a flavour of its social role, then you are better off trying to see how it is used rather than simply grabbing a pocket dictionary and looking it up. For a word like 'culture', a word that is constantly being fought over, mobilised for different ends, and inflected with a range of ideas, it clearly won't be enough just to look at one or two examples of how the term is used and how it has been used.

Dictionaries, especially the large multivolume ones, do have their place though and can be particularly helpful in revealing the various historical permutations that the word culture has gone through. For instance, in the 2002 fifth edition of the *Shorter Oxford English Dictionary: On Historical Principles* (which runs to 3,750 very large pages of dense text divided into two volumes) the entry for 'culture' provides seven different meanings for the word. The first two meanings relate to agri*culture* and are found from about the twelfth century (the Middle English Period in dictionary periodisation). Culture then referred to a piece of land to be cultivated. This was the first recorded meaning for the word – its original meaning. This meaning gets a new twist in the late nineteenth century (the third meaning) when it could refer to a medium (a culture) for growing spores or cells. The fourth meaning dates from the early sixteenth century and expands the agricultural referent and transfers it to the human subject through a metaphorical extension. Culture became a way of cultivating improvements in manners and mind through training and education. So if you could cultivate a field to make it produce valuable materials, metaphorically you might want to think of education offering a similar preparation to the mind. In the early nineteenth century (the fifth meaning) this was extended further to include intellectual and artistic artefacts (books, paintings, music) that could be seen to store refined and tasteful practices. It could include works deemed worthy by those who claimed they had refined taste. Thus it wasn't until the middle of the industrial revolution that you had the association of culture with books and other artefacts. Finally in the mid and late nineteenth century it expands again to include the achievements of a particular society at a particular stage (meaning six) – for instance, Renaissance culture or the culture of the Enlightenment. And then finally (for my dictionary) it opened up again to include all the 'distinctive customs, achievements, products, outlook, etc., of a society or group; the way of life of a society or group' (meaning seven) (2002: 575).

These seven meanings can be grouped into three sets of distinctive meanings, the first of which is largely either redundant or only used as part of a specialised vocabulary, while the second two are very much in evidence today. I will refer to these three general meanings throughout the book, particularly to definitions two and three. So culture means:

1. The activity or phenomena of growing or tending to something. Culture in this sense is not often used today but its trace can be found in words like agri*culture*, horti*culture* and is still used

to refer to the culture you could find in a petri dish for growing bacteria or in terms such as tissue culture. But in the sense that it is concerned with growth and nurturing it feeds into the second meaning.

2. Culture is seen as a form of *cultivation* for the mind and for the citizen (as lessons in taste, in manners, in art, in intellectual endeavour). In its most selective form it is synonymous with 'high culture', a highly selective set of artefacts and practices often chosen by an elite (by tastemakers, for instance, such as gallery owners, or those with the power to shape curricula). This is culture as a very particular form of *evaluation* and is used when someone asks, for instance, if a person is *cultured*. A famous example of this position is in the writings of Matthew Arnold. In his book *Culture and Anarchy* in 1869 he wrote 'culture is, or ought to be, the study and pursuit of perfection; and that of perfection as pursued by culture, beauty and intelligence, or, in other words, sweetness and light, are the main characters' (53) – or more succinctly, culture is 'the best which has been thought and said in the world' (5). Today, I think, few people would have a sense of 'the best which has been thought and said' as an uncontested terrain (there is no reason to assume that Arnold did either), but many might have a sense that Shakespeare is more firmly part of culture than Beyoncé even if they prefer Beyoncé. In its choice of objects this meaning of culture is also keen to associate culture with expressive and representational forms such as books, films, music and so on.

3. The most expanded meaning of culture is as a 'way of life'. This is the meaning of culture that is primarily associated with the way that it is used in ethnography and anthropology. In E.B. Tylor's *Primitive Culture: Researches into the Development of Mythology, Philosophy, Religion, Language, Art, and Custom* (of 1871) he famously introduced his book by writing: 'Culture or Civilization, taken in its wide ethnographic sense, is that complex whole which includes knowledge, belief, art, morals, law, custom, and any other capabilities and habits acquired by man as a member of society' (1). It covers an extensive list of areas of social life and is clearly aimed at attending to the totality of a way of life as meaningful and as materially practised. While

this meaning was initially associated with a technical language of the emerging social sciences (particularly anthropology) it found a strong footing in ordinary language. Today, for instance, in a free newspaper with a thematic listing of 'tonight's TV choices' the thematic categories include: drama, comedy, fun, soaps, factual, culture, sport, and film. Under 'culture' there is no sense of Arnold's 'the best which has been thought and said', instead there is a list of reality television with such titles as *Storage Wars*, *Mum of the Year*, *First Dates*, and *Invasion of the Job Snatchers*.

My sense is that when I first started studying culture (in the early 1980s) the second definition was more dominant than the third (within the world at large, that is). People expected culture to be *improving* to some degree, or they had a sense that this was the meaning of the term. Today I have a feeling that it is the third meaning of culture that is more dominant, and perhaps this is partly due to the way that reality television has popularised a very loose sense of ethnographic culture.

From dictionary searches we can get a quick snapshot of a word undergoing enormous amounts of change across a long period of time. But this transformation isn't the swapping of one meaning for another, rather it is the complexity that arises when quite distinct and to some degree incompatible meanings co-exist (as you can see above my examples for meaning two and three are situated within two years of each other). So today it is possible that two people who work together, for instance, might be using the term culture to refer to quite different phenomena. One could be using the term as a form of judgement, using it to legitimate a claim for something as 'refined' or valuable, while someone else will not be attaching an evaluation to their use at all, simply pointing to that vague terrain of life that can include food, manners, clothing, styles of talk, news-papers, music, and so on. But this sense of the word 'culture' changing over time and now pointing to quite different phenomena is only a very broad introduction to what is both so hugely seductive and so problematic about this word. To get a sense of the dynamism of how the term 'culture' is used we need to throw ourselves into some more particular and complex articulations of the term.

In this chapter, by way of an introduction, I'm going to look at two examples where the word 'culture' is not so much defined as set to work. The first case comes from government. The UK government, like many other governments around the world, has a department dedicated to culture. In the case of the UK it is called the 'Department for Culture, Media and Sport'. Given that such departments not only offer powerful meanings for their terms but are also instrumental in deciding what sort of practices and institutions will receive funding and what will not, they are crucial realities that we have to face in constituting a world of culture. The second example is to look at the way the term is used in publishing and in the titles of books, loosely academic books, that have 'culture' in the title, not just as an explicit object of study but as a qualifying approach to the study of a specific phenomenon. I have chosen fairly randomly from thousands of possible titles that claim to be about the culture of this or that. So my interest will be in looking at what happens when a book is titled *The Culture of Knitting*, rather than say *Knitting: The Basics* or *Advanced Knitting*. What sort of a qualification is this and how does it prepare us in advance for the sorts of things we are likely to find within it, while also warning us about what will not be included so as to avoid possible disappointment for those wishing to improve their knitting techniques? Treating the term culture as a form of qualification is useful for getting a sense of the sort of functionality the word has today. So rather than assuming it points to a realm, or a particular set of objects, the term might have more to do with the way we approach specific realms and objects. At the end of this chapter I will also look at the dangers that we are facing when we employ the word culture, and to suggest ways of addressing these dangers.

## 'CULTURE' AT THE DEPARTMENT FOR CULTURE, MEDIA AND SPORT

Most governments around the world have something like a ministry of culture. For instance, the ministry of culture in Estonia includes various departments and undersecretaries within it that go on to further spell out the large terrain of culture. In Estonia then the ministry of culture includes divisions of fine arts, cultural heritage, international relations, cultural diversity and sport. Iran has a ministry of Culture and Islamic Guidance. Italy has a minister of Cultural Assets and Activities. We don't even need to invoke China's 'Great Proletarian Cultural Revolution, 1966–76' (normally just shortened to 'the cultural revolution') to insist that the State in some form or other has an important role to play in the way that the term culture is used, and in effecting and affecting the forms of culture that a population are exposed to. Looking at a particular instance of governmental work around culture is also a way of clarifying some of the particular and peculiar aspects of the way that 'culture' operates today.

Here I am going to be looking at the way 'culture' functions for the 'Department for Culture, Media and Sport' (DCMS) in the UK. On the main internet portal (Gov.uk) to the DCMS, the department represents its mission in the following way:

> The Department for Culture, Media & Sport (DCMS) is here to help make Britain the world's most creative and exciting place to live, visit and do business. We protect and promote our cultural and artistic heritage and help businesses and communities to grow by investing in innovation and highlighting Britain as a fantastic place to visit. Alongside this, we protect our deeply held beliefs in freedom and equality. We help to give the UK a unique advantage in the global race for economic success.
>
> (DCMS website 2015)

Creativity, excitement and heritage might be the terms that stand out as connected to culture. But we should also note the insistent emphasis on business and perhaps the unusual sense that this department is going to 'protect our deeply held beliefs in freedom and equality'. We shouldn't expect such a statement to offer a neutral account of 'culture', after all it is a government department under the control of a political party (in this case an alliance between two UK parties: the Conservative Party and the Liberal Democrats) and we should assume that this statement will reflect their values and interests, to some degree at least.

The institutions that the DCMS sponsors give us more of a sense of what 'culture' could mean in the context of the British state (and are less contingent on the ideologies of the particular parties in power). These institutions include the Arts Council England, the British Film Institute, the British Library, the British Museum, English Heritage, the National Gallery, the Natural History Museum, the Science Museum Group, and the Tate. These are museums, libraries, galleries, and funding bodies that have a broadly educational remit and are mostly dedicated to the act of selecting particular items as significant and valuable (with the exception of the British Library which famously attempts to exhaustively collect all publications). These are institutions that would fit with the second definition of culture in that they are involved in acts of 'cultivation' – storing and supporting that which is seen as most important for history, or the best, most refined examples of art, and so on. In an old-fashioned sense you might make use of these institutions if you were aiming at 'improving yourself'.

As important institutions sponsored by government they could be seen as involved in legitimating phenomena as 'cultural' in the restricted sense that definition two offers. A gallery like the National Gallery or the Tate is involved in selecting sets of artefacts which then (precisely because they have been selected) become seen as the best examples of visual art. This is in many ways a self-legit-imating and tautological process: the Tate is tasked with collecting the best art; the best art is what is collected by an institution such as the Tate. Art collections are perhaps the best-known examples of the selective tradition of high culture.

But to look at culture, *as a process*, it is more interesting to take institutions whose objects might initially have had little to do with what is usually taken for cultural practices (the world of paintings and sculptures, film, novels, theatre, music and so on). At least in these non-cultural examples the edges of what constitutes the cultural can be seen more emphatically. What are we to make, for instance, of museums like the Natural History Museum or the Science Museum? Aren't they dedicated to precisely those things that culture is not: science and nature? Why is the DCMS spon-soring these institutions? And given that within the agencies of the British government there is a 'Government Office for Science' (GO-Science) that attempts to 'ensure that government policies

and decisions are informed by the best scientific evidence and stra-
tegic long-term thinking' (GO-Science website 2015) what would be
the difference between the science you find in the Science Museum
and the science that is circulating in the offices of GO-Science?

The most obvious answer here is that what makes science cultural
is *time*. Both the Natural History Museum and the Science Museum
plot a history of landmark discoveries across centuries of scientific
endeavour. They offer up a history of science as a heritage of
discovery, of adventure (and misadventure) and as exotica. The
science that GO-Science presents to the government is not represented as the latest chapter in this history. The science GO-Science
champions is based on quite a different set of qualities and
values: this is scientific knowledge that purports to be at its most
robust, reliable and verifiable. So we could say that what the scientific community (as represented by GO-Science) understands about
climate change today will find itself being part of science history
tomorrow. To shift from science-as-science to science-as-culture,
all it would have to do would be to wait around a bit.

This example, very crudely drawn no doubt, opens up a problem
that will be continually addressed in this book. Science is both
culture and not culture. Nature is both culture and not culture.
Engineering is both culture and not culture. Violence is both culture and not culture. And so on. Culture, because it can encompass
what is educational, what is experienced and what is part of daily
practice, is capable of encompassing the entire spectrum of
human endeavour (the complex whole of life) including much of
what is clearly not cultural for those who practise it, and is not
cultural in terms of its ambitions and values, or in terms of its
phenomenal form. Tautologically there is nothing in the known
world that can't be known, thought about, perceived, represented
(however adequately or inadequately). And it is this *human* aspect
that is cultural. A rock might be just a rock, it might be best studied
by a geologist who might have the best chance of explaining its
existence, its morphology, its natural history. But because a rock
is a thing that can be 'known' and represented (by geologists,
poets and bulldozer drivers) it enters the world of culture, as does
the geologist in her or his attempt to explain it. This ability to
absorb everything is both the most emphatic problem with culture

and culture's most productive and ambitious characteristic. So for a religious believer, believing in God is not something that belongs to culture, it is something that belongs to religion. But precisely because believing in God is a practice that alters from one religion to another, because it is practised in special buildings fitted-out with particular ritualistic equipment, and because it involves people who have specific roles within the practice of a religion, we can claim these aspects as *cultural*. Just as we can talk about the culture of a hospital and the culture of medicine without claiming that what a surgeon is doing when they remove your appendix is 'doing culture'.

This is clearly a problem that needs some clarification and in the chapters that follow I hope to clarify this without losing the ambition of culture to attempt to apprehend the 'complex whole'. But there is no critical power to attending to something as culture (in the anthropological meaning of the term) if we can't also recognise that 'culture' is not a set of objects or phenomena (or not just a set of objects or phenomena) but is a way of apprehending and attending to a set of objects and phenomena. To have a sense of the productivity of attending to the world through the optics of culture we also need to constantly remind ourselves that it is precisely an optic, and not the only one available. While the expansive nature of 'culture' is unprecedented it is not a perspective that is likely to uncover new energy sources, find a cure for cancer, or provide food for the starving. Culture as a terrain of investigation is limited in its power. It might however be invaluable in alerting us to how energy is experienced and imagined, it might help us come up with better ways of thinking about cancer and how to relate to illness and death, and it might provide a valuable perspective for understanding something about the global unevenness of food distribution.

To return to my example of the DCMS we can see that for the most part the second meaning of culture as improvement and cultivation is most functional for this government department and the institutions it sponsors. Some of the institutions (such as the National Gallery) might have a very strong sense that they are holders of the 'best which has been' rendered (in paint, bronze, charcoal, clay, and so on). Other institutions might have different priorities that might include, not the 'best', but the most important or influential inventions and discoveries. But there are other institutions besides museums and arts organisations that are sponsored by the DCMS. The DCMS sponsors, for instance, the Equality and Human Rights Commission. This is hard to link to any of the meanings of culture that we have looked at so far. Yet it clearly connects to an important aspect of the DCMS's policy priorities. For the year 2013 they set out their priorities in the following way:

In 2013, our priorities include:

creating a fairer and more equal society, including opening up marriage to same-sex couples

helping to provide a lasting legacy for the 2012 London Olympic and Paralympic Games (working with the Cabinet Office and colleagues across government)

supporting vibrant and sustainable arts and culture nationally by continuing to fund arm's length bodies like the Arts Council, giving incentives to the creative industries and by sponsoring the UK city of culture programme (Derry – Londonderry in 2013)

helping roll out the next generation of mobile communications (4G) and working to transform the UK's broadband network by 2015

sponsoring ongoing national and international campaigns promoting UK tourism

(DCMS website 2015)

While the rolling out of a faster broadband network and helping instil a legacy for the 2012 Olympic and Paralympic Games might relate predominantly to media and sport (which of course can be absorbed into a cultural perspective) it is the idea of 'creating a fairer and more equal society', as well as the notion of a 'city of culture' and the relationship to UK tourism, that are worth noting. None of these three priorities fits with the dominant definitions of culture that I've been looking at so far. None of them fit straightforwardly into the sense of Matthew Arnold's 'the best which has been thought and said'. Yet they aren't straightforward examples of the more anthropological definition of culture either. The anthropological sense of culture, in its most ordinary form, suggests that culture covers the terrain of meanings and practices belonging to a way of life. The examples from the DCMS's list of priorities suggests a different 'take' on culture, one that is evaluative without relating to 'high culture' and one that is keen to intervene in social life.

One of the meanings of 'culture' that isn't taken into account by my dictionary is the sense of culture as it relates to something like the Equality and Human Rights Commission. This is a meaning of culture where the sense of culture in its anthropological meaning (as a complex whole) folds back to the initial meaning of culture as 'tending', 'caring', 'cultivating' and 'nurturing'. Under the banner of all sorts of 'cultural' activities (cultural policy, cultural politics, cultural improvement, cultural rights, etc.) culture has become a central arena for understanding inequality, discrimination, forms of non-physical violence and so on. It has also, as is clear from the DCMS's mission statement, become a key area for economic growth. Of course a group of people campaigning for the inclusion of minority languages within a school curriculum is significantly different to a regional tourist board trying to 'sell' the delights of a particular area to holiday-makers. And yet both of these groups could be seen to be 'tending' to social and material life, to 'nurturing' a relationship towards a heritage, a landscape and a tradition.

This meaning of culture seems to blend the three meanings of culture together in a vague and powerful way. So, for example, the idea that to go about 'creating a fairer and more equal society, including opening up marriage to same-sex couples' (something that was achieved in March 2014 in England and Wales) might be a cultural act (rather than a primarily social or political act) has all the evaluative elements of meaning two combined with the anthropological (meaning three) sense of culture as an arena of 'belief, art, morals, law, custom', but with a strong sense of intervening in this cultural terrain.

To take another example. The UK City of Culture programme has, on the one hand, a fairly restrictive understanding of culture as constituted primarily by the arts and what is often called the heritage industry (including museums, historical buildings, monuments, and so on). This is how the DCMS briefed potential applicants for the title of UK City of Culture 2017 (a competition that was won by the city of Hull):

> Culture is generally taken to include the following areas: arts (including visual arts, literature, music, theatre and dance), architecture, crafts, creative industries, design, heritage, historic environment, museums and galleries, libraries, archives, film, broadcasting and media. We would expect to see a range of these areas included in bids and cultural programmes. In addition, you may also choose to include sport and science, but these should not be major elements of your bid and programme.
>
> (*UK City of Culture 2017*: 7)

This is clearly a version of the second meaning of culture (as coterminous with the arts) with the emphasis on areas of creative and historical content. But the objective of the UK City of Culture competition is not simply aimed at supporting creativity, rather it is aimed at urban regeneration (a form of boosterism) and a range of social goals framed by the DCMS tag-line 'improving the quality of life for all'.

It is in its social and economic objectives where you find a much more extensive idea of culture and one that is clearly coterminous with the social sphere. So applicants are asked to direct their cultural programme to what are seen as socially beneficial aims:

> The UK City of Culture 2017 will need to:
>
> Deliver a programme that uses culture and creativity to lead to lasting social regeneration through building engagement, widening participation, supporting cultural diversity and cohesion, contributing to the localism agenda and reaching out to sectors of the community who are disenfranchised and isolated.
>
> Create a demonstrable economic impact from the programme, through investment and innovation in culture and creativity.
>
> (*UK City of Culture 2017*: 6)

It is the phrase 'cultural diversity' that speaks to the multicultural reality of UK cities in the twenty-first century and ties the project to an understanding of culture provided by the anthropological definition of culture and connects such diversity with 'sectors of the community'. In this sense 'cultural diversity' is another term for 'ethnic diversity'.

The 'culture' of the City of Culture competition is a good example of how all of the meanings of culture collide as a way of extending the idea of nurturing and cultivation to an urban population and to a population of visitors. It is semantically confusing because within a single sentence culture is used to mean 'the arts' at one point and 'ethnic diversity' at another. Both meanings come together as forms of 'nurturing' that are both economic and social (bringing social cohesion to a fragmented and disenfranchised social scene). Culture as a programme of broadly artistic events (from parades and carnivals to classical concerts) is seen to be the way of achieving this nurturing in what is a post-industrial country:

> UK City of Culture is more than just a title. It's a focus, a rallying cry, a call to action, an opportunity to create and innovate, to build local pride, to show the world who you are and what you can do. It can inspire, instil a sense of ambition and provide the base for a real step change. And of course, it's a platform for a year-long celebration of local cultures and the great cultural diversity of the UK today.
>
> (*UK City of Culture 2017*: 3)

We might be sceptical about the political motivations and machinations of this programme, about the sorts of links that are being forged between commerce and the arts, or commerce and community, but as an example of the variety of ways that the term 'culture' can be mobilised I think it is exceptionally rich. It points to the confusion that the term culture has within the world today. We need to remember this real-world confusion as we go about finding productive ways of framing the term culture and putting it to work as a perspective for doing critical and scholarly work.

## CULTURE AS A PERSPECTIVE

In the following section I'm going to be analysing a few descriptions of books taken from the promotional blurbs that you find on their back covers or on publishers' websites. The books all have the word culture in the title. This is a quick way to get a sense of how culture is used as an indicator of the range and scale of an investigation. I'll start by looking at a title where culture is not the *object* of investigation but is, rather, the *mode* of investigation. This is a book (and it is one of thousands) that deploys a cultural *perspective*, and as such can be useful for giving us a quick indication of the sorts of materials and approaches that might be used in providing a cultural account of a specific phenomenon. As I mentioned above, and as a random choice to start with, I'll start with knitting and Joanne Turney's book *The Culture of Knitting*.

Book titles are designed to indicate what a book is about, what a reader can expect to find in the book, and, crucially, what the book is unlikely to include. The publisher's blurb continues this preparation, while also championing the book's contents and approach. This is the blurb for *The Culture of Knitting*:

> From booties and scarves to art and fashion, *The Culture of Knitting* addresses knitting as art, craft, design, fashion, performance and as an aspect of the everyday. Drawing on a variety of sources, including interviews with knitters from different disciplines as well as amateurs, the text breaks down hierarchical boundaries and stereotypical assumptions that have hitherto negated the academic study of knitting, and it highlights the diversity and complexity of knitting in all its guises. *The Culture of Knitting* investigates not merely why knitting is so popular now, but the reasons why knitting has such longevity. By assessing the literature of knitting, manuals, patterns, social and regional histories, alongside testimonial discussions with artists, designers, craftspeople and amateurs, it offers new ways of seeing, new methods of critiquing knitting, without the constraints of disciplinary boundaries in the hope of creating an environment in which knitting can be valued, recognised and discussed.
>
> (Blurb for Turney 2009)

From this blurb we can draw out some characteristics that might well be common to cultural perspectives more generally. A list of characteristics might include:

1. Knitting as culture is not one thing. The blurb alerts us to the idea that knitting isn't contained in a category like 'craft', but moves across a number of categories such as art, design, as well as being part of ordinary practices. Indeed while these

categories are themselves cultural (there are no *natural* distinctions between art and craft, for instance, it is a human construction), they have huge effects to what knitting *is*, how it is experienced, and so on.
2. 'Knitting' exists in lots of different sites, not just in the act of constructing something out of wool. Here the author looks at knitting manuals and pattern books, as well as talking to all sorts of knitters and finding historical evidence of knitting. Which leads us into:
3. A cultural perspective seems to invite a number of different approaches that include looking at historical changes, looking at the way knitting is practised differently in different places, and finding out how people involved in knitting feel about their work as knitters.

It might seem an odd thing to say, or a fairly obvious thing to say, but there is no mention here that by reading this book you will find out *how* to knit. There is also no reason to assume that the author Joanne Turney is herself a knitter. If we google her we find out that she is an academic working at Bath Spa University in the UK where she describes herself in the following way: 'I am a Design Historian with a keen interest in the study of the everyday and the ways in which objects inform experience, in particular the ways in which the ordinary can become extraordinary. I specialise in textiles and fashion as material culture, using an ethnographic approach to my research' (Turney website 2015). We can see from this that her interests are historical and ethnographic, and that she is interested in everyday life (suggesting perhaps that she is using both definition two and three of culture). There is no indication that she is an expert knitter – her expertise lies elsewhere (though, of course, she might be an expert knitter too, but this expertise is not necessary for her job or for her to write the book).

It would be premature to say precisely what a cultural approach is but I think we could tentatively suggest something of the following concerns could be representative of what a cultural perspective implies at the moment. (I will have much to say later in this book about how I think a cultural perspective should be developed and directed.)

1. Closeness-distance: a cultural approach seems to be interested in how a phenomenon is experienced in the world. It doesn't start out by looking for correct knowledge of something or by looking for something's essential character (its ontology, as philosophers might say) but in how that something is being experienced or how it has been experienced. It is interested in a close-up understanding of a phenomenon as it is experienced by different agents (by an amateur knitter, say, making jumpers for family and friends, or by an artist working with wool). But, although it values closeness, because it is interested in culture as an *extensive* realm it doesn't necessarily value closeness in its overarching perspective. By this I mean that it might actually be a disadvantage if you (as someone setting out to study a topic culturally) were too close to your topic. Distance is as much part of the cultural perspective as closeness is. We could say, in this instance at least, that a cultural approach works comparatively by examining a varied set of close-ups, and that it is the comparativeness that requires distance.

   If we took another example – say postage stamps – a cultural approach could be interested in looking at stamps from the 'inside' so to say (from the point of view of a stamp designer, or a stamp manufacturer, or a stamp collector, or a stamp dealer) but not from any one 'inside'. In this context being invested in one particular aspect of stamp collecting or knitting might actually be a disadvantage.

2. Stability-instability: a cultural perspective would be interested in how a phenomenon (a practice, an object, etc.) changes over time, or how it changes from one context to another, or from one group to another. It is both interested in change (for instance, how hand-knitting might have changed from being a pragmatic necessity to a luxury and a hobby) and in the way practices and their meanings are established. Which is perhaps just to say that a cultural perspective takes the phenomena it is looking at to be *dynamic* and for culture itself to be dynamic. From a cultural perspective all phenomena are potentially or actually unstable. A rock, for instance, may have existed for millions of years, but how we think about it and how we understand it is something that has changed over time. With

other more obviously social phenomena (from knitting to disease, from stamp collecting to football) it seems clear that their changes aren't intrinsic to them but are related to all sorts of other changes: for instance, you could look at the impact that industrialisation, in the form of machine-knitting, had on the practice of hand-knitting, and so on. But change is nothing without the processes by which the new takes hold, the way it gets taken up and is consolidated, by groups, by institutions, by supporting practices. If you were interested in studying something from a cultural perspective, then, you might want to choose something that is obviously unstable, that has changed and is changing, but you might not want to choose something that never had any stability as this might suggest that it never became an important part of culture.

3. Real-imagined: the evidence that can be employed for a cultural perspective is startlingly diverse. A cultural study of knitting or stamp collecting or xenophobia could use memoires, cartoons, films, novels, historical records, interviews, and so on. The cultural then is made up of the real and the imagined, and it doesn't set out to necessarily privilege one over the other, but instead to recognise that our reality, our cultural reality, is made up of the interlocking of both. So the itemised contents of a wool factory are not of any necessarily greater significance than a novel where one of the protagonists works in a wool factory. From a cultural perspective our actuality is made up of rocks and ideas about rocks, wool factories and imagined lives spent in wool factories. There are some phenomena (romantic love, or religion) that seem to exist more precisely in the world of the imagination and representation, but even such seemingly ethereal phenomena have a very real material presence in the world (the world of valentine cards, internet dating sites, and so on).

If we move to another blurb we can see precisely how a cultural perspective might best be seen as a *second-order account*: it is not primarily an account of knitting, but an account of the accounts of knitting. In this there is a certain 'meta' level of analysis. We can see this clearly in the blurb for an edited collection called

*Cultures of Natural History*, edited by Nicholas Jardine, James Secord and Emma Spary:

> This lavishly illustrated volume is the first systematic general work to do justice to the fruits of recent scholarship in the history of natural history. Public interest in this lively field has been stimulated by environmental concerns and through links with the histories of art, collecting and gardening. Twenty-four specially commissioned essays cover the period from the sixteenth century, when the first institutions of natural history were created, to its late nineteenth-century transformation by practitioners of the new biological sciences. An introduction discusses novel approaches that have made this a major focus for research in cultural history. The essays, which include suggestions for further reading, offer a coherent and accessible overview of a fascinating subject. An epilogue highlights the relevance of this wide-ranging survey for current debates on museum practice, the display of ecological diversity, and concerns about the environment.
>
> (Jardine, Secord and Spary, 1996: back cover)

*Cultures of Natural History* offers a range of accounts of different moments, different formations of natural history across six centuries. It is concerned with change but also with stability and importantly with the way that certain versions of natural history become institutionalised through phenomena such as museums and university departments. It uses the plural of 'culture' partly to indicate that it is going to be looking at a number of instances of relatively stable formations. So culture as a perspective allows us to move from natural history to the history of natural history and to the practices, beliefs, institutions of natural history as they change and are stabilised.

My last blurb differs from the other two as this one is not about a cultural perspective on a particular phenomenon but takes as its object of study 'culture'. The book is by a professor from a business school and the book is titled *The Culture Map*:

> Whether you work in a home office or abroad, business success in our ever more globalized and virtual world requires the skills to navigate through cultural differences and decode cultures foreign to your

own. Renowned expert Erin Meyer is your guide through this subtle, sometimes treacherous terrain where people from starkly different backgrounds are expected to work harmoniously together. When you have Americans who precede anything negative with three nice comments; French, Dutch, Israelis, and Germans who get straight to the point ('your presentation was simply awful'); Latin Americans and Asians who are steeped in hierarchy; Scandinavians who think the best boss is just one of the crowd – the result can be, well, sometimes interesting, even funny, but often disastrous. Even with English as a global language, it's easy to fall into cultural traps that endanger careers and sink deals when, say, a Brazilian manager tries to fathom how his Chinese suppliers really get things done, or an American team leader tries to get a handle on the intra-team dynamics between his Russian and Indian team members. In *The Culture Map*, Erin Meyer provides a field-tested model for decoding how cultural differences impact international business. She combines a smart analytical framework with practical, actionable advice for succeeding in a global world.

(Meyer 2014: Blurb)

To be clear, Meyer's book is aimed at the business community, it is aimed at senior managers working with international teams, or with buyers and sellers who are faced with a global market. My point here is that its perspective is *not* a cultural perspective in the way that it is for the previous two books: it isn't interested in exploring the stability and instability of practices and categories across time and across space. It has a particular goal in mind: to increase cross-cultural communication in the interests of global business.

The result of this is a process, at least from the point of view of the blurb, of ultra stabilisation: the Germans, Israelis, French and Dutch are blunt; Americans are overly positive; Asians and Latin Americans operate with a complex hierarchical attitude, and so on. There are problems here, and we encounter them in everyday life all the time: we call them stereotypes. I'm not interested here in either condemning or condoning stereotypes, that isn't the point of this example. The point is that 'culture', as a set of assumed particularities, is always going to be something that a cultural perspective has to deal with: in a very real sense it is the medium of the cultural. But a cultural *perspective* would see these categories as produced, unstable, open to contestation by different groups, dynamically related to other contexts, stabilised via institutions (including business institutions), and so on. But this blurb precisely isn't offering a cultural perspective on culture, it is offering a more instrumental perspective or a more pragmatic one, and in doing so the anthropological sense of culture is fixed and unified as a reified set of meanings and forms.

In this book I'm going to be navigating between these very different uses of the term culture, between culture as a perspective and culture as an object, between culture as a set of evaluations and culture as an attempt to grasp the complex whole. I don't promise any answers (the issue runs too deep for that) but I hope I can offer some clarification, and some productive and complex areas for further investigation. But before I end this introduction it is worth, from the start, itemising the problems with 'culture', both as a perspective and as an object of study.

## THE DANGERS OF CULTURE

Within this initial sketch of the uses of the term culture there should be enough to suggest that 'culture' brings with it as many problems as solutions, as many dangers as productive ways forward. Here I'm just going to suggest three dangers that I think are worth being aware of, and which might make those who attend to the cultural dynamics of the world more modest in their claims. In writing this book I want to promote the value of culture (I teach cultural studies, so I have a vested interest in this), and I want students and researchers to be ambitious about what it means to attend to the cultural, but with this necessarily should come a sense of humility, a sense that there are limits to culture. So here are my dangers ...

1. *Superficiality.* I'm not sure if this is a danger or just something to recognise. Finding out about the culture of something does not necessarily result in knowing that something (you don't become a knitter in studying the *culture* of knitting). In some instances this is just as well – there is lots of cultural work to

be done on unpleasant aspects of life. But it does mean that a cultural perspective isn't as profound as we sometimes like to think. Because a cultural perspective is interested in what is often most changeable in it, it is often overly concerned with the outward surface of phenomena, with the way that a practice presents itself. I think a cultural perspective has to take this on. Sometimes it will have to sacrifice the scale of culture's perspective for something more involved and involving. Take the example of the cultural study of religion: what is missing is probably the one thing that characterises it – what it is like to have faith, to believe. (This will become clearer in later chapters.)

2. *Inflation.* One of the dangers that occurs when you attend to the world as culture is that you can quickly assume that there is nothing else out there. Because everything (or an aspect of everything) can be absorbed within a cultural perspective it is easy to make the mistake that nothing exists outside of culture. There is a truth in this, but it is a shallow truth because it is based on a tautological logic. It goes something like this: culture deals in meanings, the only meaningful things are meanings, therefore the only meaningful thing is culture. A strong cultural perspective (a mistaken one I believe) may defend this position by saying: 'You may say that the world is made up of chemicals and energies, that it smells and vibrates, but I say to you that these chemicals and energies are only meaningful when you name them, when you give them meaning and insert them into a language.' This over-inflates the role of culture, and severely deflates the role of the material world in the shaping of the world and how we experience it. There are clearly a myriad of things that exist in the world before we name them as such and lots of phenomena in the world that we are having a hard time absorbing into culture. A cultural perspective needs to be modest enough to see this and ambitious enough to work in those areas that are least agreeable for a cultural perspective (climate change, death, and so on).

3. *Exoticism.* The global bank HSBC ran a series of adverts a few years ago telling the world it was a globally aware bank. In many ways it was the forerunner of a book like *The Culture Map*. It persuaded you that to live in a global world it was

necessary to know the customs of the countries you were visiting so that you would know whether you were being offensive
or not. In one sense it was telling us to learn good manners in
our global wanderings (if wandering is what we do). But in
another sense what it offered, and what it still offers, is a series
of extreme juxtapositions of cultural differences as spectacular
culture. For instance, in a television advert for HSBC we are
shown a group of Chinese businessmen entertaining an English
businessman at a restaurant. The Englishman eats a dish of
cooked eel that he seems not to be enjoying, but he finishes the
plate of food. At this another larger eel is cooked for him and
the other diners. Again he looks queasy but finishes the plate.
At this an even larger eel is cooked. And so it goes on. The
voice over states: 'The English believe it is a slur on your host's
food if you don't clear your plate, whereas the Chinese feel you
are questioning their generosity if you do. At HSBC we never
underestimate the importance of local knowledge. HSBC, the
world's local bank.' This is the sort of culture that you get in
*Lonely Planet Guides*, or *Rough Guides*, it is the view of the
tourist who doesn't want to cause offence. I think that a cultural
perspective can actually encourage this gaze. It sensitises perception towards difference and extremes, but without normalising
them within a social world.

It is worth keeping hold of these dangers throughout this book.
I'll try my best to assuage some of them or at least to address them
and to see if there is productivity in them. In the next chapter I
am going to look at the explanatory power of culture. In other
words I am going to ask what it means to explain a phenomenon
by claiming that it is culturally determined, which will also mean
asking about other forms of determinism.

# 2

---

# LANDSCAPE

Like many words, the word culture picks up meanings not just through the associations and characteristics that the word is seen to exemplify, but also in opposition to a range of other words. So, for instance, culture takes on meanings from words that are very close to it ('society', 'the arts', and so on) but also from words that are often defined as its opposite ('nature', 'science', etc.). Of course, as we have already seen, 'culture' has an extraordinary ability to absorb everything in its wake, so much so that to talk about 'the culture of science' or 'the culture of nature' is neither a contradiction nor a rare occurrence in the general study of culture. It is telling, though, that while 'nature' can be used in a very loose way (so that saying the 'nature' of something is no more than saying what it is like) the phrase 'natural culture' is an unusual construction, used to promote CDs of 'spiritual music' or African-like robes made from natural fabrics.

One of the ways of investigating a key term like 'culture' for an area of intellectual inquiry (in this case the field of media and cultural studies) is to ask about the term's ability to explain the phenomenal world. What is the *explanatory power* of 'culture'? What can it explain that other terms (such as 'nature' or 'science') can't quite explain? And, alternatively, what are the limits of a cultural explanation? What can't it quite explain? I think that a cultural perspective can often explain a good deal, but it often falls short of being able to explain initial causal factors. For this it is often necessary for a cultural explanation to rely on something else – for instance to connect to biology or to call on 'the economy' or on contingency, or some other realm. This is not to see the cultural as having some sort of fatal flaw that means that we need to become biologists, economists or exponents of the random organisation of life, and thereby have to abandon a cultural perspective. Rather it is to describe a cultural perspective in terms of its strengths and weaknesses, so that cultural forms of enquiry can play to those strengths while acknowledging the weaknesses. I hope that this chapter and the following ones are able to contribute to a mapping out of these strengths and weaknesses.

In this chapter I want to concentrate on the interactions between culture and nature in the context of landscape. In our relationships with animals, weather, and landscape we often reserve the qualifier 'wild' to designate phenomena that seem to be furthest from culture or from our idea of culture. So while we might have pet dogs and cats such animals quickly become very different beasts with the epithet 'wild'. A wild dog conjures up an animal that is dangerous and unpredictable, likely to bite and maim and spread diseases. Weather is 'wild' when wind and rain threaten to cause damage, when its effects cannot be managed. The landscape is 'wild' when there are no signs of human habitation or farming. A wild landscape might include mountains or craggy hills, sparse plains, deserts or rain forests: these are uncultivated and unpeopled landscapes – a wilderness.

Yet isn't our very idea of the 'wilderness', of wild nature, or nature in the raw, also conveyed through novels and films, through institutions like national parks or conservation areas? Doesn't our sense of the furthest reaches beyond culture come from poets and adventurers who have somehow represented the wildness of the wilderness for us? Deploying a sense of culture capable of absorbing everything in its wake, the late environmental activist Alexander Wilson wrote:

Nature is part of culture. When our physical surroundings are sold to us as 'natural' (like the travel ad for 'Super, Natural, British Columbia') we should pay close attention. Our experience of the natural world – whether touring the Canadian Rockies, watching an animal show on TV, or working in our own gardens – is always mediated. It is always shaped by rhetorical constructs like photography, industry, advertising, and aesthetics, as well as by institutions like religion, tourism, and education.

(Wilson 1992: 12)

It's a foregone conclusion: you can't escape culture, ever. 'Nature' is a cultural construct. And saying this is to take note of the way that we imagine snow-capped mountains or frozen tundra or 'the jungle' *through* paintings, novels, travelogues, metaphors, and such like. 'Nature' is there, already, in our imaginations. And even when we stare, slack-jawed, in front of a canyon in Arizona, we are already filled with 'views' seen of canyons and canyon-like land-scapes. Sometimes the 'real thing' isn't quite as good as our filmic memory, because we have no abilities for dramatic close-ups, no ability to render swooping aerial camera movements (hence the popularity of the helicopter rides through the Grand Canyon to help render 'nature' more vividly).

Recognising that nature is part of culture is a way of insisting on the presence of history, of politics, of human decision making and agency. Likewise to refuse culture and to think of nature as *natural* (if you can forgive the tautology) is to avoid a slew of determining factors as to the form that our perspective on nature takes. For Alexander Wilson, 'to say, for example, that radioactive isotopes – radiation, in everyday language – are a natural occur-rence is to hide the economic and political decisions taken about nuclear power development' (Wilson 1992: 13). To claim nature as natural (unsullied by human factors) is to avoid recognising human factors which will always be present as soon as a phe-nomenon is part of the human world. We can see this in land that has been cultivated by human husbandry; it is less evident in parts of the world that have not been 'spoilt' or cultivated by human endeavour (though knowledge of human-induced climate change makes this more and more unlikely). To see something as natural (be it radiation, sexuality or children) is the first step in seeing something as unchangeable and unquestionable. There are lots of very good reasons for insisting on the culture of nature.

But just as 'nature is part of culture', so too, perhaps, there is a nature (a wildness) that *escapes* culture. So perhaps culture is a word that *seems* to encompass phenomena, but is *really* describing a specific aspect of phenomena. Perhaps culture is that which is most readily available for scrutiny, or that which most readily enters into the world of representation. But even if we stick to this world of representation does this mean that we exhaust what comes into our world as 'nature'? Have we really grasped our encounters with the Arctic and Antarctic when we say that it is inescapably entangled with stories of polar expeditions and heroic acts of self-sacrifice such as Captain Oates' walking out into a blizzard in 1912 ('I am just going outside and may be some time') as he knew his ill health was jeopardising the British Antarctic expedition? Are the extreme regions of polar exploration part of culture, or do they insist on something other than culture, something unmanageable, wild, and deadly? Even that which is outside 'culture' is (paradoxically) capable of being incorporated back into culture, precisely as wild culture, and uncontrollable nature.

This is a paradox that is played out again and again and is part of our modern condition. It is a central aspect of writing the wild. One of the most famous examples of writing the wild is Jack London's 1903 novel *The Call of the Wild*. The novel is the story of a dog (Buck) who is living as a pet in California, but is stolen and taken to the Yukon area of Canada to become a working dog, pulling sleds and working for gold diggers. After his final owner is killed the dog returns to its 'natural' state and answers 'the call of the wild'. The novel is seen from Buck's perspective and charts the way he has to relearn his primal nature (and unlearn his cultivated behaviours) within the packs of pulling-dogs that he is put in (where 'dog eats dog', literally as it turns out). The book could be seen as an articulation of a core wildness that is intrinsic to even the most domesticated animals. It is an argument that many pet owners know when their precious kittens start presenting them with dead birds and the like. Yet in Jack London's novel we also have the paradox that this 'truth' (that nature exceeds culture) is presented in a novel, written by a man who imagines the consciousness of a dog, and that this novel and other representations like it provide us with cultural representations that filter into a collective imagination of what it means to be 'wild'.

In what follows I want to explore the relationships of nature–culture by looking at the dual processes whereby culture (the results of human endeavour) is naturalised to become part of nature and the way that nature (in this instance the 'wild' landscapes of US National Parks) is turned into culture. I also want to try and clarify how we can deal with the paradox that that which is outside or exceeds culture can also be seen as being part of culture. By returning to the three definitions of culture and by imposing limits on the realm of culture I think we will get a better understanding of where a cultural explanation ends and where other sorts of explanations need to be called for (even if these other explanations have a cultural aspect to them).

## CULTURE INTO NATURE

One of the central aspects of culture, in the ethnographic sense, is that cultural conventions don't reveal themselves as 'cultural' to those whose conventions they are. It is often what others do that is most obviously cultural, and what you do that is natural, normal, just common sense. We can learn quite quickly that the food 'we' eat, and the way that 'we' eat it, is just as much a cultural convention as the ways and manners of groups who eat in very different ways. The small differences that exist between cultures that share the same language and a good deal of similar heritage (for instance between British and American) make vivid the contingent nature of manners. For instance Americans (or at least right-handed Americans) tend to cut up their food and then eat it with the fork in their right hand; the British (or at least right-handed Britons) tend to eat their food with the fork in their left hand, cutting it up as they go. It would be bizarre to say that one style was more natural than the other. But if you've always operated in one way it will feel 'natural' to you, while the other styles will seem like a convention that you are adopting.

Our own cultural styles are the cultural forms that seem most natural, least cultural. Habit here has an enormous role, allowing conventions to become automatic responses, making manners appear normal, allowing forms of thought to be seen as 'common' sense. Sometimes we can only see our cultural world through the eyes of others, or by looking at historical changes and trying to imagine what it was like to live before such conventions existed. Naming common practices as cultural makes them visible in a particular way, gives them a history and a determining set of circumstances (the invention of cutlery and crockery, the emergence of conventions of etiquette, the rise of the middle classes, etc.). But it doesn't make them necessarily *feel* any less natural.

Making culture appear natural is the process that generates culture as culture (as a way of life). Sometimes we can look at these conventions and think 'so what' – you drive on one side of the road, they drive on the other, you kiss each other on the lips, they hug and shake hands. You say tom-aye-toe, I say tom-argh-toe. But when conventions appear as not just *a* way of living but as the *best* way of living, the correct way, the natural way, we can see the power that culture exerts when it is dressed as nature. When a set of conventions become the standard against which all other conventions are measured and seen as lacking, or as perverse, then we are encountering a powerful force in the world, and one that is essentially ideological. When only one form of loving and living is seen as natural and all others are seen as odd, or perverse, or unnatural, we are in the realm of culture at its most powerful, political, violent and ideological.

For the French cultural theorist Roland Barthes writing in the 1950s, the foundational act of myth (Barthes' name for ideology, a name that usefully reminds us of the importance of anthropology for making such processes visible) is the way that 'it transforms history into nature' (Barthes 1973 [1957]: 129). For Barthes ' ... the most natural object contains a political trace, however faint and diluted, the more or less memorable presence of the human act which has produced, fitted up, used, subjected or rejected it' (Barthes 1973 [1957]: 143–44). What myth (or ideology) does is obscure this trace, rendering it invisible. What we don't see in the world of myth (which is the world of culture-as-nature) is the historical, social and political processes that form the object world as something meaningful. This can be a physical process; it is always a discursive process:

> Every object in the world can pass from a closed, silent existence to an oral state, open to appropriation by society, for there is no law, whether natural or not, which forbids talking about things. A tree is a tree. Yes of course. But a tree expressed by Minou Drouet is no longer quite a tree, it is a tree which is decorated, adapted to a certain type of consumption, laden with literary self-indulgence, revolt, images, in short with a type of social *usage* which is added to pure matter.
>
> (Barthes 1973 [1957]: 109)

Minou Drouet was a child writer who came to prominence in the mid-1950s as the eight-year-old author of sentimental poems, that many people believed must have been written by her mother (she proved them wrong by writing poems under observation). In 1957 she published a book of poems titled *Arbre: Mon Ami* ('tree: my friend'). The point Barthes is making is that 'a tree' might exist quite simply in the world as a material object but is also subject to discursive acts that render it as an image, a representation, as a sign (for instance the idea of 'family tree', the 'tree of life'). A rose is simply a flower ('a rose is a rose is a rose' as Gertrude Stein would say, forcing the tautology in on itself), but a rose is a declaration of love. When culture (romantic love, for instance) becomes nature we tend not to see how conventionalised this is and just see the romantic symbol. At any rate it is almost impossible to disentangle the 'pure' material object from the layers of discursive imaginings (which might include imaginings that are scientific as well as poetic, religious as well as horticultural).

Trees, plants, and landscapes are not just phenomena that are open to discursive use, they are often the result of some form of physical human activity. When we see a landscape of gentle rolling hills, made up of fields, hedges, and woods, and see this as 'nature', what we stop seeing is the history of cultivation, the history of culture becoming nature. The political philosophers Karl Marx and Frederick Engels make this point in their critique of Ludwig Feuerbach's materialist philosophy which they saw as limited:

> He [Feuerbach] does not see how the sensuous world around him is, not a thing given direct from all eternity, remaining ever the same, but the product of industry and of the state of society; and indeed, in the sense that it is an historical product, the result of the activity of a whole succession of generations, each standing on the shoulders of the preceding one, developing its industry and its intercourse, modifying its social system according to the changed needs. Even the objects of the simplest 'sensuous certainty' are only given him through social development, industry and commercial intercourse. The cherry-tree, like almost all fruit-trees, was, as is well known, only a few centuries ago transplanted by *commerce* into our zone, and therefore *by* this action of a definite society in a definite age it has become 'sensuous certainty' for Feuerbach.
>
> (Marx and Engels 1970 [1846]: 62)

Feuerbach is interested in the material world rather than a world conceived and directed by god (religious idealism), but for Marx and Engels he stops short of seeing the material world *fully* materially as a historical world, where landscapes have been fashioned through years of cultivation and human activity.

In this context the role of critical thought is to reverse the process of turning culture into nature. Critical enquiry starts out with a scepticism about the inevitability of nature: it asks how did we end up with this specific landscape? What forces fashioned it? What interests shaped it? The cherry-tree in Marx and Engels' account is also the myth-tree in Barthes' account: as long as we don't ask questions about the tree's history, the way it's imagined and the way it is used, we stay in the realm of myth. It goes without saying, of course, that *all* cultivated trees and plants that are used for food have been changed from 'wild' nature: many have been relocated across oceans, all have been tended in a way that wouldn't happen without human intervention.

Critical enquiry then means putting history into any apprehension of the material world as a way of reversing the process of naturalising culture. This act of reversing the process of naturalising culture becomes even more important when it has been directed at the cultural practices of human groups as a way of concocting a 'natural order' of human achievements and practices. In the late

nineteenth century a powerful way of talking about different societies on the planet was to see them as similar to evolutionary changes
in animals. Darwin's theories of evolution, whereby the phenotypes
of animals and plants incrementally change over successive generations allowing for very slow adjustments to the environment, was
applied to human beings suggesting that this was how humans
had evolved too, and that the different groups of humans that make
up the planet are at different stages of development. Of course the
difference here is that Darwin was connecting this to changes in
the body, not to changes in material practices and social forms of
living.

One of the most ardent believers in the 'nature' of human
evolution in terms of human achievements and human societies
was the anthropologist, collector and professional soldier General
Pitt-Rivers. For Pitt-Rivers the material culture of *his* contemporary
culture was the pinnacle of evolution. It was the result of generations
and generations of technological adjustments, from basic axes and
knives through to complex industrial machinery. Charting this
developmental line was primarily the responsibility of archaeology.
So just as preserved animal skeletons and their fossilised traces
could tell the prehistory of animal evolution, buried axes and belt
buckles could tell the prehistory of contemporary human endeavour. But alongside archaeology, anthropology was employed on
the understanding that a contemporary 'under-developed' culture
was equivalent to a now developed culture from the past. In this
way anthropology was about uncovering cultures from the past
that existed in the present.

The mistake that Pitt-Rivers made was to see technology as a
universal form, operating as an equivalent in all human societies,
as if all of humanity was working towards the fashioning of
industrial machinery for mass production. The racial and racist
dimensions of this line of thinking quickly became evident when
a contemporary culture (say an aboriginal culture in Australia) is
given a historically non-contemporaneous position in a line of
development. It wasn't hard to make the leap from placing the
technological development of a culture on a line, to thinking of
the people of that culture (and the people whose culture it was) as
somehow 'backward' in developmental terms. Such thinking was

the foundation of many of the ideologies that percolated around colonialism, and was a foundational myth of the so-called 'white man's burden' (whereby colonialism isn't seen as a structured form of exploitation of human and natural resources, but as the moral responsibility of white culture to modernise non-white culture).

Pitt-Rivers had the idea of producing a spiral-like museum that could show the evolution of human nature as one continuous evolution of human achievement through material artefacts (clothing, tools, weapons and so on). The spiral of the museum's layout would take you from the earliest (or most rudimentary) tools through to tools contemporary with Pitt-Rivers' own culture. Such cultural arrogance already presumes that culture (his culture) has become naturalised as the natural order of things against which other cultures are measured and shown to be lacking. But in deploying an evolutionary model of material culture it is also presented as a lesson to all those groups who might desire radical change in order to pursue their interests or to defeat inequalities. In the twentieth century and twenty-first century this mythic (ideological) position has been used to perpetuate undemocratic forms of government (with the idea that a people are not 'ready' for democracy, etc.). In Pitt-Rivers' time it was used as a powerful ideology against forms of revolutionary change that might produce fundamental changes in the orchestration of society. This is his rationale for his museum (a museum that never materialised, though the collection is now housed in Oxford in a museum with his name attached to it):

> It is true that the history of laws, customs and institutions cannot be displayed in museums. You cannot place the successive links of development side by side in such a manner as to appeal to the eye; but the material arts are capable of such an arrangement, and the knowledge acquired in the one branch will be, to some extent, available in the other. The law that nature makes no jumps, can be taught by the history of mechanical contrivances, in such a way as at least to make men cautious how they listen to scatter-brained revolutionary suggestions. The knowledge of the facts of evolution, and of the processes of gradual development, is the one great knowledge that we have to inculcate, whether in natural history or in the arts and institutions

of mankind; and this knowledge can be taught by museums, provided
they are arranged in such a manner that those who run may read.

(Pitt-Rivers 1891: 116)

The ideology of human evolution works to maintain uneven distribution of power between classes, genders, between different
ethnic cultures. This, to be clear, should not be seen as the goal of
a culturally oriented anthropology. Yet it is also clear that it has
been. As the critical anthropologist Johannes Fabian wrote, 'an
evolutionary view of relations between Us and the Other is the point
of departure, not the result of anthropology' (Fabian 1983: 104). In
other words when anthropologists start out from the position that
contemporary cultures exist within non-contemporary time
frames, they are deploying an ideology, not pursuing empirical
investigation. The ideology of the 'law of nature' is a powerful
way of turning culture into nature. To be told that 'this is how
humankind progresses' is just another way of being told to 'know
your place' whether you are a worker, a woman, a colonised people.
A developmental hierarchy of social groups has been a crucial
aspect of most dominating forms of society everywhere, and has
been their rationale and alibi for subjecting people to the tyranny
of culture.

## NATURE INTO CULTURE

But just as cultural interpretations and social arguments have
become transformed into nature (into laws of nature), there has
also been a concerted effort to transform nature into culture. In
one sense this is the story of culture in its most original sense of the
term: the story of husbandry and horticultural cultivation. The
'taming' of nature has marked the distance between a hunter-gatherer
society and a more settled agricultural society. But the wild landscapes where we imagine hunting-gathering to have been practised,
and the groups of people who lived by hunting and foraging have
systematically been ruined by colonising cultures.

How we see landscapes, wild or not, may itself be cultural in terms
of perception. This is what William James means by appercep-
tion, that storehouse of imaginings and perceptions that already

exist prior to seeing something for the first time. Landscapes are seen through collective eyes (cultural eyes) that have been taught to appreciate certain kinds of views that have been associated with the picturesque and the sublime, for instance. In this there is not an innocent eye that is seeing the world for the first time, but an eye trained in its apperceptions. The art historian Nicholas Green wrote about landscape in a way that brought this aspect into the foreground:

> I am looking through the train window. The view is, for me, hypnotic: the sky a deep impenetrable blue; open fields receding in gentle undulations, equally intense under the slanting beams of a low January sun; the bare branches of an occasional tree spread-eagled against the sky, fingering the blue. In the distance, the black dense copse seems precisely placed to frame and close the panorama, while above a flock of birds – rooks perhaps – wheel and circle, following the line of some invisible tractor. [ ... ] As if the glass of the window becomes the two-dimensional surface of a picture on which are traced the lines of successive planes. As if nature itself becomes the means of its own objectification.
>
> (Green 1990: 2)

Green recognised that the view he was seeing was itself informed by a myriad of images. Many of these belong to culture in the sense of a selected tradition of paintings and literature that have been used to establish a set of cultural values. It would be wrong however to imagine that this is simply the preserve of high culture (a culture reserved for an elite). We find the pictorial compositions that were made in the eighteenth and nineteenth century everywhere: on calendars, as the basis for garden designs, in tourist attractions, in photographs that people take of landscapes and so on.

(In the 1990s Komar and Melamid, a pair of Russian-American artists, arranged for a market research firm to survey thousands and thousands of people across the globe to find out what kind of paintings were the 'most wanted' and what were the 'least wanted'. Based on the outcomes of the survey which asked detailed questions about size, content, colour, style, and so on, Komar and Melamid painted a pair of paintings for each nation. The most wanted paintings were nearly always a wilderness scene, often with an animal in it, and sometimes, incongruously, a historical national figure [George Washington, say]. The project was called *Painting by Numbers: Komar and Melamid's Scientific Guide to Art*, and while it was clearly intended as a humorous provocation [the resultant paintings fitted no ones' description of what anyone in particular wanted] it did show the extent in which a generalised image of an 'unspoilt' and bountiful wilderness, modelled on nineteenth-century representations, circulated throughout the world. [See Wypijewski 1999.])

In nineteenth-century North America the idea of preserving an 'unspoilt' landscape from commercial encroachment and habitation became a campaign which led to the foundation of various national parks (Yosemite, Yellowstone, and the Grand Canyon being the most famous) and the establishment of a governing body for US parks called the National Park Service in 1916. The emergence of a conservation movement for natural landscapes in America is impossible to disentangle from the colonisation of America by European settler communities whose aim was towards the ownership and cultivation of a landscape that had for centuries been a landmass 'occupied' by indigenous peoples who were destroyed by colonising forces. In the enterprise of settling a North American landscape the idea of an unspoilt landscape was not something that was becoming a scarce resource, indeed 'unspoilt' landscape was a problem to overcome rather than one to preserve:

> The initial American attitude toward the environment paralleled that of the Old World from which it sprang. Preserving wilderness for public benefits, the national park idea was perhaps the last thing the colonists desired. Their problem was too much rather than too little raw nature. Wild country had to be battled as a physical obstacle to comfort, even to survival. The uncivilized hinterland also acquired significance as a moral wasteland, a dark chaos which civilization and Christianity would redeem and order. The original American mission had no place for wilderness.
>
> (Nash 1970: 727)

The idea of preserving large areas of landscape as a wilderness didn't come from people who were engaged in trying to cultivate that landscape or people who were trying to establish settled life, nor did it come from the indigenous populations who were being driven off their land as they had no voice in such negotiations. It came instead from city dwellers on the east coast who travelled to the west as quasi-tourists. One of the first champions of a national park idea was the painter George Catlin, who made his livelihood from painting indigenous first-nation Americans in their traditional dress. Indeed his initial idea was a national park that would include both landscape and indigenous people within a bounded space. For Catlin the spectacular landscapes of the Rocky Mountains, or the Great Plains of the mid-west, would make 'a beautiful and thrilling specimen for America to preserve and hold up to the view of her refined citizens and the world, in future ages! A nation's Park, containing man and beast, in all the wildness and freshness of their nature's beauty!' (Catlin cited in Nash 1970: 729). For Catlin it was the 'cultured' mind that could perceive the beauty of the wild, natural landscape: 'the further we become separated from that pristine wildness and beauty, the more pleasure does the mind of enlightened man feel in recurring to those scenes' (Catlin cited in Nash 1970: 729).

The first official national park was Yellowstone National Park which was the result of an act of government in 1872:

> The Act signed into law on March 1, 1872, established the world's first true national park. It withdrew more than two million acres of the public domain in the Montana and Wyoming territories from settlement, occupancy, or sale to be 'dedicated and set apart as a public park or pleasuring-ground for the benefit and enjoyment of the people'. It placed the park under the control of the Secretary of the Interior and gave the Secretary responsibility for preserving all timber, mineral deposits, geologic wonders, and other resources within the park. The establishment of the park set a precedent for placing other natural reserves under federal jurisdiction.
>
> (National Park Service website)

Preserving landscape as 'natural' becomes an act of government that allows and condones certain uses of the landscape (education and tourism, for instance, but also land management, animal control and so on) while outlawing other uses (exploitation of mineral resources, selling land for habitation and so on).

In the work of Richard Grusin, a cultural historian of American national parks, these parks are cultural technologies that don't passively preserve a notion of nature that is already in existence, imbedded somehow in the landscape, but actively *produce* and *reproduce* nature according to aesthetic forms that are in circulation: 'national parks were created in postbellum America as technologies for reproducing nature according to the aesthetic forms and practices of nineteenth-century landscape representation' (Grusin 2004: 172). In Grusin's study of North American national parks it is the 'discursive' forms of nature that are the parks' particular currency:

> To establish a national park is not to put an institutional fence around nature as you would put a fence around a herd of cattle. Rather, to establish a national park is to construct a complex technology, an 'organic machine' that operates according to and within a discursive formation, a set or network of discursive practices. Saying this is not to deny the matter-of-fact sense in which establishing a national park involves preserving an area of land as 'natural' as opposed to (for example) converting it into a farm, a ranch, a mine, a housing development, a shopping mall, or an amusement park. Nor is it to deny the differences between what goes on inside the boundaries of a park and what goes on outside. But these differences are not intrinsic ones, differences in the essence or 'nature' or quality of the land on one side as opposed to the other; rather these differences are the product of a complex assemblage of heterogeneous technologies and social practices, the aim of which is the production and reproduction of a culturally and discursively defined and formed object called 'nature'.
>
> (Grusin 2004: 3)

By 'discursive' Grusin means a range of 'framed perceptions' – forms of description from literary and scientific sources, government acts, tourist postcards and maps, paintings and photographs, and so on. While Grusin is keen to insist that the importance of discourse does not mean that material acts of preservation or husbandry do not matter, what does matter is that they are framed by such discursive actions which are determining of how a national park comes into being, how it is thought about, and how it is received by its visitors. In this sense 'discourse' is another name for culture as a realm of meaning. But does the discursive *explain* a phenomenon in a satisfactory way? What are its limits? Obviously in trying to explain something like Yellowstone Park there are lots of explanations we would need that wouldn't fall within the 'cultural' field (geological explanations, for instance). But to look at the limits of a cultural explanation I want to look at an example that at first glance would seem to be something that could and should be fully explainable within a cultural perspective.

## CULTURAL EXPLANATION AND ITS LIMITS

I want to use one specific painting by the British artist J.M.W. Turner as a way of testing the limits of various cultural explanations and seeing what there is beyond the *cultural* that might be useful for explaining cultural material. My fear is that once someone becomes engaged in the study of culture, there is a tendency to see the realm of culture as so all-encompassing that they may discount explanations that might exist outside of this realm, or else to see any such explanation as another layer of culture. Cultural explanations often have an unassailable authority about them which are based on the tautological premise that the only meaningful things in the world are meanings and that all meanings are acts of interpretation which are open to contestation and to historical shifts. A cultural perspective is in danger of seeing everything in the world (or everything that can be viewed culturally) as a cultural construction that must be viewed as the result of specific human interests, historical styles, and particular ways of interpreting the world. There may be critical power in this when we want to contest claims that this or that behaviour is seen as *unnatural*, for instance, but what happens when a petroleum company, for instance, suggests that the 'science' of climate change is an *interpretation* of the world, and uses the fact that climate science doesn't deal in absolute certainties to continue pushing against restrictions on the exploitation of fossil fuels? In other words what happens when a cultural perspective argument is used by those who already have power and use it to further their interests? These are questions I will return to throughout this book. For this section I have a more historical case study.

Turner was born in 1775 and died in 1851 (the year of the Great Exhibition). His art has become a cornerstone for the identity of a national artistic heritage, due in part to a number of bequests that Turner made in his will. A short list of current-day Turner-associated phenomena would include the following: one of the newest galleries in England is called the Turner Contemporary (in Margate, in Kent); the annual prize for contemporary art is called the Turner Prize; a separate wing of Tate Britain (the Clore gallery) is dedicated to the Turner bequest. Turner's reputation is not something that exists as a historical relic, but is something that circulates today. In 2014, for instance, there were two major Turner exhibitions (*Late Turner – Painting Set Free* at Tate Britain, and *Turner at the Sea* at the National Maritime Museum) as well as an award-winning film, *Mr Turner*, directed by Mike Leigh.

Much of Turner's reputation has been associated with his later work and with his depiction of atmospheric landscapes and sea-scapes, often with spectacular weather effects (sunsets, storms and so on). Indeed a dramatic sky is often called 'Turneresque'. Such aspects of his art have given it a subsequent value as being impressionistic and expressionistic and as somehow anticipating much later art movements such as Impressionism, Expressionism and Abstract Expressionism. According to the art historian Sam Smiles, an exhibition held in 1966 at the Museum of Modern Art (MoMA) in New York could be seen as cementing this particular view of Turner:

> Ninety-nine paintings and watercolours, most of them from Turner's maturity and many of them unfinished, helped position Turner at the very heart of all that seemed advanced in modern art, as though in his practice lay the origin of developments leading ultimately to Mark Rothko's evanescent abstract paintings of the 1940s and 1950s. This, however, is to view Turner with hindsight, as an honourable precursor to Impressionism or the more expressive tendencies in abstract painting, and it is a viewpoint which cannot be critically sustained.
>
> (Smiles 2000: 10)

In historical terms such a position is an anachronism. It is of course a powerfully suggestive position offering us a version of Turner as 'ahead of his time', and it has become a popular understanding of Turner's 'genius'.

Much of the subsequent critical art history (for instance Sam Smiles' writing) has worked hard to restore Turner to his contemporary context and see him as an artist of his time. So, for instance, John Barrell's recent review of Turner's 2014 exhibition at Tate Britain can celebrate Turner not as someone who is ahead of their time (whatever that could possibly mean) but as someone deeply engaged with their time:

> One of the most remarkable things about Turner's last works is how enthusiastically they engaged with the mid-19th century, its technological and economic developments, and how his painting developed in the effort to represent them [ ... ] *The Fighting Téméraire* [fig 2.1] the great image of the decline of Britain's mercantile power and of the age of sail giving way to the age of steam, as the great wooden ship is towed up the Thames to the breakers by a squat paddle-driven tug vomiting thick smoke from its iron funnel.
>
> (Barrell 2014: 35)

This is to see Turner's paintings as being somehow explainable in relation to the industrial revolution and to changes in the intellectual and material circumstances in life.

If we concentrate on Turner's painting of *The Fighting Téméraire*, we could say that one understanding of it (an understanding that operates primarily within the second meaning of culture as a selective tradition of legitimated art) is to see it as part of an art historical continuum in which art responds to art and predicts developments in art. This would be to see the painting as being 'about' the play of light and the paint effects of light on water and the abstract scumbling of sky and cloud. Another understanding of it would be one that operates with both the second meaning and the third meaning of culture (i.e. culture as the complex whole of life). This meaning could argue that to understand the painting we need to recognise that it isn't *only* about light effects and painterly bravura, but puts such techniques in the service of a

*Figure 2.1* J. M. W. Turner, *The Fighting Téméraire, tugged to her last berth to be broken up,* 1839. Courtesy of The Art Archive/ National Gallery London/Eileen Tweedy.

larger purpose, namely depicting large-scale transformations in society and culture.

It is this second explanation of the painting that is represented in an essay by the French philosopher Michel Serres titled 'Turner Translates Carnot' which was published in English in 1988 (but was written at the end of the 1960s). Serres explains Turner's painting as showing a moment of change, whereby a previous world of wind-powered commerce and movement that was based around a very exacting geometry of navigation gives way to a new source of commerce and movement powered by steam and furnaces. In his essay the ship (*The Fighting Téméraire* – whose name derives from its role in the Battle of Trafalgar) represents the old world of wind power and geometry, while the tug boat that is towing the old ship to a dock so that it can be broken up, represents the new world of fire and steam. For Serres the tug 'carries within itself a conflagration, which it both masters and encompasses, from which it draws its power. It carries in itself fire, air, and water. It is the material microcosm, the world's model' (Serres 1988: 159). The painting shows *The Fighting Téméraire* as being 'assassinated by her towing-vessel' (Serres 1988: 159). In this the painting is both allegory and actuality (the *Téméraire* was being towed by a steam-powered tug so that it could be destroyed).

But the painting is not just reducible to its putative subject matter. In his essay Serres compares Turner's paintings to paintings which could be seen to represent the age of geometry and wind. What makes Turner's painting different is not just its subject matter but its way of rendering this subject matter. So while the old ship, especially in relation to its rigging, is painted in a very precise manner, the rest of the painting is painted by someone who is keen to get the measure of this new power:

> Turner is no longer a spectator on the side-lines [ ... ] he enters the boiler, the stove and the furnace. He sees matter being transformed by fire; the world's new matter at work, with geometry cut down to size. The whole order is turned upside down, materials and paint triumph over drawing, geometry, and form. No, Turner is not a pre-Impressionist. He is a realist, or more precisely a materialist.
>
> (Serres 1988: 158)

For Serres the materialism of the painting is its capturing of atmospheric effects, but these atmospheric effects aren't about sun on water, but about a new age of power – steam. And the age of steam is a smoke-belching, exploding, conflagration of force. Such an age demanded a way of picturing that could somehow render this force onto canvas. The result is Turner's painting.

Such an explanation of the painting explains both its subject matter (why it depicted this particular event) and its peculiar way of depicting it (why it painted the event with such painterly gusto). It shows us the explanatory power of a cultural perspective that can move from a limited sense of culture (as a selected tradition of paintings, literature, and so on) to a much broader sense of culture that would include thoughts, feelings, beliefs, forms of communication, commercial practices, forms of transport, and so on.

Many years later Michel Serres returned to this painting and his essay about it and claimed that he may have been wrong in his explanation. Since his early explanation of Turner's painting new information had been discovered: 'results obtained via core samples drilled through layers of ice in the glaciers of Greenland have laid waste my old intuition, which had sprung from the history of the natural and social sciences' (Serres 1997: 10). These core samples revealed that 'in the years when Turner was painting his sooty and pyrotechnical canvases, Tambora, a 9,000-foot volcano in the Lesser Sunda Islands of Indonesia, exploded suddenly, spewing clouds of burning ash into the upper atmosphere' (Serres 1997: 10). Now Serres wonders if the particularity of Turner's painting is due to volcanic clouds of dust rather than his confronting the industrialisation of his environment, that way that he 'daubs rather than sketches. He blends rather than calculates. In so doing he directly confronts the changes in how matter and force are understood' as one of Serres' commentators has it (Brown 2002: 6).

The discovery of volcanic eruption leads Serres to doubt his initial explanation of Turner's painting:

> To be sure, Turner painted steamships and fires of all sorts, but the sieve of ashen fog that dropped like a veil between things as they usually are and his strange canvases – did this ashy screen come from the eruption of that volcano in the Sunda Islands, or from the social reflections of the Industrial Revolution? Did it come from the phenomena of nature or from the effects of society? Were the air, the light, and the sky of London direct manifestations of telluric powers, or were they indirect manifestations of relations of force remodeled by fire-driven machines and the factory proletariat? Since the immediate moves more quickly than the mediated, geophysics seems more powerful than economic history – Tambora more powerful than Marxist analysis. Was I mistaken? I am ready to admit it.
>
> (Serres 1997: 12)

Was he mistaken? Is the eruption of a volcano a *better* explanation than an explanation that ties his painting to the emergence of the full force of the industrial revolution? Does the volcano trump and obliterate the other explanations in terms of its truthfulness and its materiality?

What Serres is offering is not a final explanation, but a provocation about explanation. He doesn't suggest that an interruption by nature (the volcanic eruption) *necessarily* invalidates other forms of explanation but he does wonder what kind of an explanation there could be that might want to discount the volcano as a materially determining factor in how Turner fashioned his picture. Could there be a third explanation, one that incorporated both positions? Was the volcanic cloud that came between Turner and the towed ship recognised as a force of nature that allowed Turner to represent something of the force of the industrial revolution? Perhaps. The point for us should be that culture does not necessarily have the full range of possible explanations even of cultural material.

Serres ends his reflection on 'the case of Turner' by asking that those in humanities and social sciences need to take more account of the forces of nature, just as those who deal in science need to take account of social and cultural consequences and determinations:

> Experts in economic history take no account of plate tectonics, and specialists in glaciology couldn't care less about sociology. Even as they renew the idea of time's percolating flow, geophysicists ignore history; even as masses of people die in earthquakes or eruptions, geophysics leaves historians indifferent. In short, society is not concerned with nature, and nature is even less concerned with society. The dialogue does not take place. By proclaiming loudly that the fine arts, like mental illness or scientific discoveries, are socially determined, do we keep ourselves from hearing the thunder of even volcanoes? On the other hand, how many epistemologies have not heard the noise of Nagasaki? In physics, an experiment has no social effects. Scientific ideas must deafen us, if we can hear neither eruptions nor atomic bombs! In the first of these two cases, social science forgets climate – the atmosphere itself and its opacities, the earth and its instabilities. In the second, indifferent to humanity, the hard sciences seem to ignore war, its murders and its miseries, and death, received or given.
> (Serres 1997: 16)

It is a profound provocation and suggests that much of what goes by the name today of interdisciplinarity is really just an internal conversation amongst those involved in the human sciences. The real 'inter-discipline' will have to jettison the either-or explanations available. We will have to overcome the choice of either science or culture, either nature or culture to find some other way of discussing the world. This means that the explanatory power of *both* culture *and* science will need to be qualified, questioned and contested.

Such a rapprochement between nature–science and culture may be some time off. In the meantime though we can make some headway on preparing the ground for such interdisciplinarity by recognising the strengths and weaknesses of a cultural perspective and showing that within certain bounds forms of cultural explanation do not necessarily shut the door on other kinds of explanation but can open up the terrain. To get there I want to return to the third meaning of culture as it emerged in anthropology and to show how the ambition of anthropology still offers us an extraordinary invitation to map the relationships between phenomena.

# 3

## A WHOLE WAY OF LIFE

In the introduction I pointed out that two powerful understandings of culture (culture as a set of values embedded in manners, books and works of art, and culture as an ethnographic ensemble that might add up to a 'whole way of life') developed into significant meanings simultaneously in or around 1870. The historical simultaneity of two quite distinct meanings for the same term (one evaluative, one descriptive; one restricted, one extensive) requires some explanation.

If we take the case of England in the period from the mid nineteenth century to the end of that century (and the anthropologist E. B. Tylor and the poet Matthew Arnold were both English) then we can see a number of changes that would have affected the way that the two meanings gained traction. In the second half of the nineteenth century England and Britain more generally witnessed a number of developments in technology (the massive expansion of the railways, for instance), in geography (the expansion of its imperial reach), in industry (which combined technological and financial developments), in communication (the growth of a national newspaper industry), and so on. It is worth focusing on two developments as having particular importance for how 'culture' was being thought and rethought.

The first development we need to consider is the massive growth in literacy that occurred during the second half of the nineteenth century:

> English literacy rates, measured by marriage register signatures, almost doubled in the final sixty years of the Victorian era. In 1840, one-third of all bridegrooms and one-half of all brides made a crude mark on the marriage register; by 1900, around 97 percent of all grooms and brides signed their names. This marked improvement in literacy levels coincided with the establishment of a national system of elementary schooling.
>
> (Bailey 1994: 89)

Such enormous growth in literacy was not simply the result of a national system of education, it was also the outcome of people moving to cities and of education becoming part of industrial culture (workers received education in writing and arithmetic through a variety of organisations run by workers' associations and by philanthropic commerce). Literacy was part of the promise of being modern.

Alongside the growth of literacy there was also a massive increase of printed material to read: this was the great age of the national newspaper as well as a myriad of regional versions; it was the age of public libraries and libraries attached to charitable organisations. And it was an age when folk culture or 'popular culture' (culture 'made by the people for the people', as the saying goes) grew and eventually became a thriving industry (and to some degree lost its connection to ordinary cultural producers). 'Culture' as 'the best which has been thought and said' was in competition with a popular culture that was seen by some as the 'worst that can be thought and said':

> In the 19th century, 'penny dreadful' was an unofficial literary category – used by its enemies and its fans to describe cheap serial fiction produced in weekly eight or 16-page instalments, which might, in the course of months or even years of publication, supply rambling

narratives founded on poisoning, strangling, burglary, flagellation and hairbreadth escapes from drowning and sexual assault. Their titles generally gave away their natures: *Varney the Vampire; or, The Feast of Blood* (1845–47); *Wagner the Wehr-Wolf* (1846–47); *The Night-Hawks of London; or, the Noble Highwayman and the Miser's Daughter* (1865). The semi-literate – who made up an important part of their market – were reeled in by the lurid woodcuts: Black Bess, rearing against the moon; the heroine, bare-breasted and manacled in a burning attic; a bloodsucking fiend scuttering over a four-poster bed.

(Sweet 2014)

Culture, as a selective tradition of 'civilised and civilising' books, emerged within a landscape that was saturated by all sorts of commodities. Culture as a value of refinement and civilisation was a bulwark against the possibilities of a culture that was available to all and also one that might encourage debauchery, low morals, and lack of deference to 'elders and betters'. (The present day 'penny dreadful' – in terms of how they are imagined – might be various reality TV programmes, or computer games like *Grand Theft Auto*.)

The second phenomenon that undoubtedly impacted on the way that the term culture was used and understood is the growth of international trade and the imperial reach of Britain and other colonial countries during the second half of the nineteenth century. This period reconfigured the world in terms of trade, transport and geo-politics:

British economic success in the late nineteenth century rode on the back of the colossal growth in world trade whose value increased tenfold between 1850 and 1913. British enterprise was still better placed than any competitor to promote this expansion of trade and profit from it. Technology (especially the application of steam power), capital (accumulated from industrial and commercial success), institutions (already developed to serve a highly integrated industrial and commercial economy) and personnel (both commercial and technical) equipped it to exploit overseas opportunities all over the world.

(Darwin 2009: 114)

International trade (what, today, we would call globalisation) and the colonial forms that accompanied it transformed the world. Countries such as India (which only exists as a nation state as a result of such transformations) were extensively 'administered' by Britain: this meant that those elements that an anthropological understanding of culture sees as central (beliefs, laws, language, customs, etc.) were transformed in the process. British culture was extensively deployed across the subcontinent, clashing and inter-mingling with cultural forms that were already established. British 'culture' was disseminated via a British colonial police enforcing British inflected laws; an Indian school system transmitted British history and taught the English language, and so on.

During this period national cultures were packaged (unevenly, of course) as discrete and consumable 'brands'. Geography, tourism and commerce concocted powerful sets of images (image repertoires) for a country such as Ceylon (now Sri Lanka) as a lush landscape made up of mountains and fertile soil out of which endless tea plantations spring forth (as part of nature, rather than industry). In the images the plantations are tended by colourfully clothed women, who seem to be luxuriating in the landscape rather than working the land. These mythical image repertories were perpe-tuated by the work of advertising and promotion agencies like the Empire Marketing Board. They deploy the idea of culture as 'a whole way of life' (hugely truncated), and mythologise that life as part of nature rather than culture (no sign of violent plantation managers, no sweating bodies toiling on the land, no financial motivations).

The second half of the nineteenth century also saw the birth of one of the most significant symptoms of global modernisation: the World's Fair (also called International Exhibitions, Expos and such like). World's Fairs contained the 'whole world' in small bundles of produce and culture – they were a snapshot of inter-national relations with some countries reduced to a few signs of indigeneity while other countries were presented as bastions of invention, thought and achievement (home to what was imagined as 'the best which has been thought and said'). Needless to say that such displays were orchestrated by those with imperial ambitions and colonial interests. Perhaps the most telling of such image-repertoires were 'peopled exhibits' – exhibits that revolved around living displays of 'natives' undertaking various routines within vernacular settings (peasant dwellings). For example:

> The Chicago Columbian [Exhibition of 1893] boasted the widest range of peopled displays shown anywhere up to that time, and the trend continued to move upward. Apart from the seventeen villages [including Dahomey, Chinese, Javanese, Soudanese, Alaskan, Arab, South Sea Islanders and Algerian] and the Cairo Street [with sixty different ethnically specific shops and a Mosque], there were Chinese and Japanese tea-houses, a Moorish Palace, an Indian school, a Persian coffee house, a Japanese bazaar, a Parisian café, a French cider press, an English pub (the White Horse Inn), a South Sea Islanders canoeing lake, Highland Pipers, a hunter's cabin and the Buffalo Bill Show.
>
> (Greenhalgh 2011: 147)

This sort of popular anthropology (or anthropology as freak show or exotic consumption) was one of the ways that 'culture' as a cosmology of rituals, practices, material culture, and beliefs was widely disseminated. Culture, in this everyday sense, tended to be what other people had. Recognising your own everyday life as 'culture' required a way of making your own world 'other'. But culture as popular anthropology was a vast simplification, reducing complex wholes into visible signs of difference, and exotic signs of otherness.

## PATTERNS OF LIFE

Anthropological notions of culture percolated throughout society on the back of newspaper reports, exhibitions, magazine articles, lectures, and popular books. One such book was James Frazer's *The Golden Bough: A Study in Magic and Religion*, first published in 1890. Frazer was a Victorian anthropologist who studied human-kind but without travelling much. His information came to him through correspondence with missionaries working in colonial outposts, from published accounts and from knowledge he had picked up from experiences in Britain and Europe. For instance, across a few pages in *The Golden Bough* Frazer can discuss ritualistic practices for rain-making and take in examples from Samoan village life, the practices of Apache 'Indians', various tribal practices in New South Wales, Australia, practices in Snowdonia in (old) Wales, and examples from Southern Europe, West Africa, China and Russia (pages 15–19).

Frazer's anthropology is an attempt to synthesise what he deems to be primitive religion which he finds in history (mythical history as much as more verifiable history), in contemporary peasant life in Europe (calendar festivals and rites-of-passage rituals) and non-industrial cultures across the globe. Frazer's project was hugely influential, suggesting a general logic to superstition and religion. Much of it has subsequently proved to be untrustworthy: but what matters for the use of the term 'culture' is that it popularised the notion of culture as a systematic cosmology of rituals and beliefs, and it finds evidence for such cosmologies *everywhere*.

Across the twentieth century there has been a powerful association of the word culture with the idea of 'pattern'. What Frazer was finding was a similar *shape* to various ritual practices and the beliefs associated with them – he was finding patterns within and between social groups. Culture in this sense is related to habit (what people do habitually in response to events, to the seasons, to everyday activity) and to symbolism (what such practices *stand for*, what they symbolise). One of the most emphatic statements connecting culture to pattern is Ruth Benedict's *Patterns of Culture* first published in 1934. For Benedict culture is a series of habits (of mind and body) that take a definite shape (like a collective fingerprint):

> The life-history of the individual is first and foremost an accommodation to the patterns and standards traditionally handed down in his [or her] community. From the moment of his birth the customs into which he is born shape his experience and behaviour. By the time he can talk, he is the little creature of his culture, and by the time he is grown and able to take part in its activities, its habits are his habits, its beliefs his beliefs, its impossibilities his impossibilities. Every child that is born into his group will share them with him, and no child born into one on the opposite side of the globe can ever achieve the thousandth part.

(Benedict 1989 [1934]: 2–3)

For Benedict 'culture' is transmitted by a community that edu-
cates the child (both formally and informally) through schooling,
by example, and through language. For Benedict we *grow* into
culture in quite a literal manner.

But there are some distinct differences between Frazer and
Benedict that not only point to the changes in the profession of
anthropology (Benedict undertook fieldwork, for instance), but point
to conceptual differences that are, I think, still hugely important
for thinking about culture today. For Frazer patterns were found
across communities: in *The Golden Bough* a rain-making ritual in
Europe might be different from one in Australia or Russia, but
the pattern highlights a similarity which suggests that the Russian
peasant might, potentially at least, *understand* (on some intuitive
level, or on a formal level) the rain-making ritual of an aboriginal
tribe in Australia. For Benedict the opposite is true: cultural
patterns are what make two communities so completely distinct.

For Frazer the differences that exist are between pre-modern
societies whose worlds are shaped around superstition, and modern
rational society. For Benedict, as it was for her teacher Franz Boas,
the different patterns of culture suggested a series of distinct cultural
shapes that could not be judged by a set of values that existed
outside of such shapes. For Boas and Benedict anthropology was
essentially a globally democratic undertaking aimed at revealing
ideas of inherent cultural superiority as a form of racism.

If both of these positions understand culture to be 'a whole way
of life' rather than the 'best which has been thought and said' then
we are entitled to ask what constitutes 'the whole way of life'? If the
'way' of that phrase is the pattern of culture, then the 'whole life' is
the life of those who share these patterns. For Benedict this is a
community, for Frazer this is 'primitive culture'. As we shall see
throughout this book the boundary of culture matters a great deal
to how we talk about culture and is something that is continually
argued over. What is 'a' culture, in this anthropological sense? Is it
human culture? Is it national culture? Is it the culture of a distinct
community (a community distinguished by class, or by belief)?
Could there be female culture? Or queer culture? Are the patterns of
culture symmetrical, or are they jagged and wild? If we can talk
about Victorian culture as something distinct from Edwardian

culture or modern culture, then how do we mark the transitions from one state to the other? Do we want 'culture' to be the name we give to fully coherent systems, or to more contradictory, fractured and fragmented phenomena?

We have here a number of arguments, but at the centre of them there is a firm belief that culture is both what connects people (there could be no culture of 'one') and what disconnects people (Frazer's culture pits 'primitive' against 'modern'). Throughout the twentieth century (and into the present) one of the most important arguments about culture within Britain (but elsewhere too) was connected to class. The way that class and culture were configured sounds distinctly contradictory. One version of the configuration might suggest that because of the class structure in Britain there isn't a single British culture but a number of quite distinct class *cultures*. Another version of the configuration might suggest that the central characteristic of culture in Britain is its class system which would suggest that British culture includes within it conflicts, division and multiplicities. We could say the same thing about gender, namely that gender inequality is a feature of British culture, so that divisions and non-symmetrical experience is a common feature.

But this is also where another problem lies. Britain, unfortunately, isn't the only country that exhibits gendered values and class divisions. Indeed these could be seen to be *the* distinctive character of macro cultural forms such as patriarchy and capitalism. Does this mean that we can talk about 'capitalist culture' and 'patriarchal culture' in the same way, perhaps (but with a very different tone), that Frazer and E. B. Tylor could talk about primitive culture? As a general rule I would suggest that there is no clear answer here, mainly because 'culture' does not exist as a naturally bounded realm out there in the world. 'Culture' as an object is, in one essential way, *created* by the person who wants to see a pattern of similarities and distinctions. If you do not see gender differences and structures of sexism, then patriarchal culture will be an irrelevant category to you; you simply will not see patriarchy. If you do not recognise patterns of exploitation and privatisation at work, then capitalism will be a mysterious way of seeking patterns of culture. Categories, of course, have to connect to an actuality that exists, otherwise they do not have any purchase on experience, but that actuality is always edited in the act of categorising it. So to categorise a set of experiences and materials under the heading of 'British culture' is itself a cultural act. Similarly to suggest that there is such a phenomenon as 'football culture' is an act of categorisation. The productivity of such categories cannot be assured in advance, only in the practice of analysis and description. (For what it's worth, I think that any attempt to name culture as *simply* a unifying category that erases conflict and contradiction is always a mistake for analysis. It might be useful for promoters and tourist boards but it is not productive for the practice of critical analysis.) So rather than think about the best units of culture it might be preferable to look at what happens when 'culture' (as a categorical unit) is deployed and what sort of uses it is put to.

One of the authors who made the phrase a 'whole way of life' a definition of culture (taken from Tylor's notion of the complex whole) was the poet T. S. Eliot who in 1948 published his book *Notes Towards the Definition of Culture*. Eliot was born in America but became a British citizen, and he was also a practising Christian. His book shows the influence of *The Golden Bough* (some of the examples come from Frazer's book) and operates with an ethnographic sense of culture as incorporating beliefs, manners and customs alongside poems and paintings. But Eliot is also concerned with culture as value. Interestingly Eliot doesn't follow Arnold in suggesting that culture must operate by including only the best that has been thought and said. For Eliot culture (as a vital and vibrant way of life) would include: 'Derby Day, Henley Regatta, Cowes, the twelfth of August, a cup final, the dog races, the pin table, the dart board, Wensleydale cheese, boiled cabbage cut into sections, beetroot in vinegar, nineteenth-century Gothic churches and the music of Elgar' (1962 [1948]: 31). Much of this has little connection to today's culture, even if you are British: who knows what 'the twelfth of August' means? You would be hard pressed to find a pin table; many dog race tracks have disappeared (my local dog track became an IKEA store at some point in the 1990s). If people around the world are at all familiar with Wensleydale cheese, then it is probably known through the animated films of *Wallace and Gromit*.

Eliot's concern was in maintaining a vibrant culture (or what he thought of as a vibrant culture) against (what he saw as) the flattening hand of a postwar welfare socialism (in this his list of characteristic cultural events was already a form of nostalgia). For Eliot religion and social differences (class) were needed to produce culture. But for culture to be vibrant and healthy for Eliot didn't mean that it had to be elite, it meant that it should have a distinctive style: 'If we take culture seriously, we see that a people does not need merely enough to eat (though even that is more than we seem able to ensure) but a proper and particular *cuisine*: one symptom of the decline of culture in Britain is indifference to the art of preparing food. Culture may even be described simply as that which makes life worth living' (Eliot 1962 [1948]: 27). Clearly Eliot was politically conservative and conservatism often has a huge stake in arguments about culture because it sees culture as a stabilising force and thereby as a way of preventing radical change. Yet within his conservatism his ideas can appear radical and socially inclusive, especially in an era where 'culture' is measured in terms of finance and profit. For instance, in broadly agreeing with a writer who argues that the 'culture of industry' should include ways of understanding how an industrial process relates to the world he adds some extra ingredients:

> Of the culture of an industry, which she believes quite rightly should be presented to the young worker: 'it includes the geography of its raw materials and final markets, its historical evolution, inventions and scientific background, its economics and so forth.' It includes all this, certainly; but an industry, if it is to engage the interests of more than the conscious mind of the worker, should also have a way of life somewhat peculiar to its initiates, with its own forms of festivity and observances.
>
> (Eliot 1962 [1948]: 16)

In this context cultural progress includes recognising connections to nature (raw materials), to global relations, to history and invention and so on. It also includes, for Eliot, forms of festivity, of ritual celebration (a rain-making ritual, perhaps). If this had included learning about the division of labour it would not have seemed out of place in a communist pamphlet on collectivisation. Perhaps such a 'culture of industry' is practised by the workers at Google?

A few years later another literary figure took up the mantle of ethnographic culture in the name of pursuing both cultural analysis and for thinking about how culture can be an arena for progressive thought and action. Raymond Williams, unlike Eliot, directed his energy towards social and cultural change and one of the ways he attempted to do this was by insisting that the two meanings of culture (as a whole way of life, and as a term that designates the arts in general) had to be combined:

> A culture has two aspects: the known meanings and directions, which its members are trained to; the new observations and meanings, which are offered and tested. These are the ordinary processes of human societies and human minds, and we see through them the nature of a culture: that it is always both traditional and creative; that it is both the most ordinary common meanings and the finest individual meanings. We use the word culture in these two senses: to mean a whole way of life – the common meanings; to mean the arts and learning – the special processes of discovery and creative effort. Some writers reserve the word for one or other of these senses; I insist on both, and on the significance of their conjunction. The questions I ask about our culture are questions about our general and common purposes, yet also questions about deep personal meanings. Culture is ordinary, in every society and in every mind.
>
> (Williams 1958: 4)

For Williams, as a literary critic as well as a novelist, the value of culture (and of the arts in particular) could not be neutralised via ethnographic distance. Culture was the pulsing life blood of communities positioned in relations of power within society. For Williams, then, class was an invitation to rethink culture as something ordinary and vital and something connected to forms of representation that could contest the status quo. Culture was always in a dynamic historical process: new feelings were always emerging and old ones were declining; new dominant forms were being challenged or were becoming cemented in institutions.

Williams grew up on the Welsh borders in a working-class community of miners and railway workers. A commitment to class politics resulted in a lifelong championing of forms of culture that could also be seen as progressive and counter-cultural (countering the cultural hegemony of the dominant class). He was a founding member of what was called the New Left in the 1960s, which was a form of socialism that took culture more seriously as a realm of struggle. It was in his book *The Long Revolution* (1961) that Williams argued most systematically about the way culture could be used as a form of analysis. In a long review of this book, the historian E. P. Thompson suggested that for a socialist, culture could never be a whole way of life, rather it was a 'whole way of struggle' (Thompson 1961: 33). For Thompson class antagonism was the essential driver of history (Thompson published his monumental *The Making of the English Working Class* a couple of years later in 1963), and culture was essentially animated by such struggle. We could say then that for Thompson the class system produced quite distinct cultures that were constantly caught in a struggle, or a clash of cultures. For Williams, social history might reveal moments of emphatic struggle, but often culture was precisely the sphere where conflict was processed as some sort of provisionally ordered disorder and settlement:

If someone were to define culture as a whole way of life excluding struggle – that would clearly have to be met with the sharpest opposition and correction. On the other hand, it seemed to me that there was a blurring between two kinds of formulation which were in fact used almost interchangeably on the left – 'class conflict' and 'class struggle'. There is no question that class conflict is inevitable within capitalist social order: there is an absolute and impassable conflict of interests around which the whole social order is built and which it necessarily in one form or another reproduces. [ ... ] Any socialist account of culture must necessarily include conflict as a structural condition of it as a whole way of life. Without *that* it would be wrong. But if you define the whole historical process as struggle, then you have to elude or foreshorten all the periods in which conflict is mediated in other

> forms, in which there are provisional resolutions or temporary compositions of it.
>
> (Williams 1981: 135)

The arguments of this debate still inform how we think of culture, though class politics are now often reworked and rethought as issues of gender, sexuality, 'race', age and religion. Indeed in the US class politics are often unavoidably 'racial' in that the working class in the United States is often visibly identified as African-American or Latino/a. But the form of these debates still revolves around the issue of whether culture is a coherent cosmology that might or might not clash with other instances of culture, or whether the 'complex whole' of culture includes within it dynamics of conflict around such animating differences as class, gender, sexuality, race, and today, more and more, religion.

In the next section I want to look at what it means to investigate culture as a coherent cosmology (of sorts) that *also* sustains differences and antagonisms. The cultural system or cosmology I will focus on is dirt.

## DIRT AS A CULTURAL SYSTEM

The potential of an anthropological understanding of culture offered to industrial societies in the twentieth century and beyond was a sort of mirror that would reflect not the image that modern western society already saw of itself, but the culture of industrialised life seen from an elsewhere or an else-when, one informed by the idea that this pattern is not anymore natural or unnatural than some other pattern. This was a form of cultural relativism that is indebted to anthropologists like Ruth Benedict:

> To the anthropologist, our customs and those of a New Guinea tribe are two possible social schemes for dealing with a common problem, and in so far as he [or she] remains an anthropologist he is bound to avoid the weighing of one in favour of the other. He is interested in human behaviour, not as it is shaped by one tradition, our own, but as it has been shaped by any tradition whatsoever.
>
> (Benedict 1989 [1934]: 1)

In one of the most famous examples of what could be called anthropological self-othering the anthropologist Horace Miner published
an essay called 'Body Ritual among the Nacirema'. The article
read as if it were describing an exotic society that practises intricate
rituals of body purification. The culture of the Nacirema includes
a 'shrine' where many of the hygiene rituals are performed:

> While each family has at least one such shrine, the rituals associated
> with it are not family ceremonies but are private and secret. The rites
> are normally only discussed with children, and then only during
> the period when they are being initiated into these mysteries. I was
> able, however, to establish sufficient rapport with the natives to examine
> these shrines and to have the rituals described to me.
>
> (Miner 1956: 503–4)

The world of hygiene rituals is not spelt out in a public forum but
is revealed in private, and often by deed rather than word.

The Nacirema, it turns out, are not some endangered tribe
attempting to sustain themselves under difficult circumstances but
are North Americans (Nacirema is simply American spelt back-
wards) whose body rituals (washing, cleaning teeth, and so on)
are performed in private bathrooms (or shrines in the article).
Miner is performing a version of cultural distancing so that
American culture can be seen within the terms of anthropology
(which favours ritual over habit, the sacred over the ordinary):

> The Nacirema have an almost pathological horror of and fascination
> with the mouth, the condition of which is believed to have a super-
> natural influence on all social relationships. Were it not for the rituals
> of the mouth, they believe that their teeth would fall out, their gums
> bleed, their jaws shrink, their friends desert them, and their lovers reject
> them. They also believe that a strong relationship exists between oral
> and moral characteristics.
>
> (Miner 1956: 504)

But Miner isn't just showing how useful anthropology can be in
providing a fresh view on our own cultural worlds (cultural worlds
that would include adverts for toothpaste), he is also making the

point that all cultures can be made strange and exotic once they have passed through the prism of anthropology. In this sense what anthropology does is not simply study other cultures but renders them exotic in the process (in a sense then this othering is the cultural work of anthropology). When anthropology is turned towards 'home' cultures, so to say, the othering continues. Thus for cultural studies, or for sociology to adopt anthropological perspectives, there is always an innate danger that it will result in what Fredric Jameson calls a 'false objectivism':

> Culture must thus always be seen as a vehicle or a medium whereby the relationship between groups is transacted. If it is not always vigilantly unmasked as an idea of the Other (even when I reassume it for myself), it perpetuates the optical illusions and the false objectivism of this complex historical relationship (thus the objections that have been made to pseudo-concepts like 'society' are even more valid for this one, whose origin in group struggle can be deciphered).
>
> (Jameson 1993: 34)

Othering may well be an inevitability when the term culture is deployed, and this problem isn't resolved by Benedict's call for a total anthropological perspective – in a sense all this does is to include 'your' own culture within the othering process. This isn't without its uses, but it is also problematic. Alternatives to such an approach will be discussed in later chapters (particularly chapters 5 and 6). For now I want to explore the 'cosmology of dirt' – particularly within metropolitan, commercial and imperial culture from an anthropological perspective and from an historical one.

The anthropologist most associated with a cosmology of dirt is undoubtedly Mary Douglas. In her 1966 book *Purity and Danger: An analysis of the concepts of pollution and taboo*, Douglas is following both Frazer and Benedict in as much as she is looking for cultural patterns and cultural logics across a huge variety of contexts. For Douglas 'any culture is a series of related structures which compromise social forms, values, cosmology, the whole of knowledge and through which all experience is mediated' (1991 [1966]: 129). This is, as you would expect, an extensive, anthropological understanding of culture, and it is a particularly useful definition which suggests that culture is not so much 'content' or 'phenomena' but *mediation* and *perspective*. For Douglas cultural ideas about 'cleanliness' and 'dirt' are ways of organising life:

> As we know it, dirt is essentially disorder. There is no such thing as absolute dirt: it exists in the eye of the beholder. If we shun dirt, it is not because of craven fear, still less dread of holy terror. Nor do our ideas about disease account for the range of our behaviour in cleaning or avoiding dirt. Dirt offends against order. Eliminating it is not a negative movement, but a positive effort to organise the environment.
>
> (Douglas 1991 [1966]: 2)

In her memorable phrase, dirt is 'matter out of place' (41) – i.e. dirt only becomes dirt when it is recognised as a substance that disorganises cultural categories (such as inside and outside).

In a chapter on the strange injunctions to be found in the Judeo-Christian book of Leviticus (part of the Jewish Torah and the Christian Bible) Douglas attempts to find a cultural logic to what at first glance seems to be a random set of instructions as to what is clean (and therefore can be eaten) and what is unclean and should be treated as an 'abomination'. For instance while cows can be eaten, rock badgers, camels, and hares are 'unclean' because they are animals which both chew the cud and have cloven feet. The instructions on what insects can be eaten goes like this:

> 20. All winged insects that go on all fours are an abomination to you. 21. Yet among the winged insects that go on all fours you may eat are those which have legs above their feet, with which to leap upon the earth. 22. Of them you may eat: the locust according to its kind, the bald locust according to its kind, the cricket according to its kind, and the grasshopper according to its kind. 23. But all other winged insects which have four feet are an abomination to you. 24. And by these you shall become unclean; whoever touches their carcass shall be unclean until the evening, 25. and whoever carries any part of their carcass shall wash his clothes and be unclean until the evening.
>
> (Leviticus cited in Douglas 1991 [1966]: 44)

Cleanliness and uncleanliness are not properties of the creatures themselves but are a result of their position within a categorical system. Insects that have wings and four legs but which crawl are disrupting the categories; winged insects that hop are behaving in keeping with the category 'flying insect'. Dirt and clean, then, are relational terms that take us to the heart of a cultural taxonomy (how the world is organised by culture).

Yet to see this as simply a set of conventions that arise out of taxonomies inherited from ancient versions of natural history is to miss the point of Douglas' insistence that culture mediates all our experience. Knowing that such injunctions about what to eat are a 'cultural construction' doesn't really reveal how such constructions can be experienced as a part of *nature* to those who have been brought up as devout believers in Leviticus, nor does it explain the bodily feelings of revulsion and disgust that might follow from mistakenly eating pork or prawns. Culture may be a form of mediation, but this mediation fashions nervous systems, gag reflexes, and alimentary canals. Culture, whatever else it is, is not worn lightly. By seeing a cultural system such as 'dirt' as deeply ingrained within sensorial experience we also get to see how deeply affecting and effective ideologies of dirt can be. When we call a joke with sexual content a 'dirty joke' or when we say someone has a 'dirty mind' we can get a sense of how far the cosmology of dirt circulates within certain cultures: when certain images or utterances make someone feel 'dirty' we can get a sense of how much passionate energy is attached to it.

To see 'dirt' as part of culture is to see culture as meaningful in that extensive sense that anthropology gives it. What connection could it have to the evaluative realm of 'the best which has been thought and said'? Interestingly concepts like dirt reveal how much evaluative material there is within the anthropological understanding of culture. Culture is freighted with ideas about goodness, about rightness, about civility. To be dirty is to be bad, to be not right, and to be uncivil. Elizabeth Shove writes that 'describing people, things or practices as clean or dirty is not a socially neutral enterprise. In use, such labels contribute to more elaborate classificatory schemes built around distinctions like those of class, race, gender and age' (Shove 2003: 88). In Britain during the second half of the nineteenth century (when the term 'culture' was getting established in its current form) 'dirt' and 'cleanliness' were deployed as ideological terms, and these ideological terms were materialised in books, images and, importantly, in commodities.

Soap is, in many ways, the modern commodity par excellence. It is a commodity that wants to live in the rational world, to be done with superstition and ritual, but it is inevitably caught up in a cosmology of dirt and pollution. In Anne McClintock's important work on the part played by soap within British imperialism – in its imagination and in its daily practices – she writes, 'from the outset, soap took shape as a technology of social purification, inextricably entwined with the semiotics of imperial racism and class denigration' (McClintock 1995: 212). She looks particularly at the advertising around soap adverts which often portrayed colonial countries and colonised subjects in their promotions. Sequences of drawings showing black children whitened through the use of soap show how racialised soap was during the period of British imperialism. For McClintock soap was animated by a range of 'good' values that went far beyond the effective removal of sweaty odours:

> The cult of domesticity and the new imperialism found in soap an exemplary mediating form. The emergent middle class values – monogamy ('clean' sex, which has value), industrial capital ('clean' money, which has value), Christianity ('being washed in the blood of the lamb'), class control ('cleansing the great unwashed') and the imperial civilizing mission ('washing and clothing the savage') – could all be marvellously embodied in a single household commodity. Soap advertising, in particular the Pears soap campaign, took its place at the vanguard of Britain's new commodity culture and its civilizing mission.
>
> (McClintock 1995: 208)

Within a cosmology of dirt, soap registered as part of cultivating culture. In this it shares elements of the two main forms of culture we have been looking at – it is a feature of everyday habits and customs *and* it is aimed at betterment. It may not be the best which has been thought and said in relation to intellectual or artistic pursuits, but it is absolutely connected to practices of the cultivation of 'good manners', of propriety.

In more recent times the connection of soap to explicit racial categories is less obvious. Today we are more likely to see soap advertising having to negotiate the modern contradiction that requires cosmetic commodities to be simultaneously emphatically natural while being manufactured through the latest scientific knowledge and technology. Today, according to the commercials, soap is concocted in laboratories by people in white coats who look through electron microscopes all day (and where the animal-testing laboratory is invisible). Today soap is associated with lush jungles and mosquito-free pools of crystal-clear water, where blonde women with long hair appear 'out of nowhere'. Is the ideological work that today's soap adverts do that different from its imperial mission? What would Ruth Benedict's child of culture learn from an extensive diet of today's soap and shampoo adverts? Is there a racial accent to these worlds of science labs and rock pools, peopled by blonde-haired beauties? Who is the cleanest of them all?

Industrial modernity has meant that cultural cosmologies are now directed by commercial forces: instead of (or as well as) Leviticus we have Unilever; instead of (or as well as) whispered instructions in bathrooms we have endless advice forums in magazines and on the internet. It is hard to imagine culture in the age of mass 'instant' communication as providing a single cosmology of belief and custom. And yet there are patterns to be found that assert themselves fairly constantly and which are hard to disengage:

> If it is language that channels our physical perceptions, it is the language of consumer products which defines our daily life. Whether we feel consciously 'for' or 'against' consumer society, the terms of our experience, the language of our delight or protest are the same. I may hold out against buying a conditioner as well as a shampoo – but I cannot wish it out of existence, or ignore the fact that it is associated with healthy, shining hair and that this is desirable. The world of consumerism is the one we live in.

> (Williamson 1986: 226)

Living in a culture doesn't mean necessarily accepting the values and beliefs that circulate most insistently within it, but it does mean that it is impossible not to be informed by these values and beliefs, and impossible for them not to shape the form of your refusals.

In many ways T. S. Eliot's sense that culture is tied to religion and that it is a form of secular-religion (however much of an oxymoron that might seem) is worth holding on to. The privileging of science and rationality, from one angle at least, must be seen as a cultic belief when it guarantees the effectiveness of a shampoo based on a clutch of Latinate words that are set to 'repair' damaged hair and add shine to lacklustre locks. In this sense the term 'cosmology' is useful for puncturing the ideology that one group of people believe in superstitions, witchcraft and totemic practices, while another group are purely rational, scientific and logical, and trade in knowledge rather than belief. As Marcel Duchamp once said, 'in general, when one says "I know", one doesn't know, one believes' (cited in de Certeau 1984: 177). Culture is that world of belief.

In mapping the logics of culture through the figure of 'dirt' Mary Douglas followed Ruth Benedict in locating patterns for culture, and in so doing offered a general approach to cultural dirt that refused to assume an innate superiority to those cultures that were most technologically mediated:

> Uncleanness or dirt is that which must not be included if a pattern is to be maintained. To recognise this is the first step towards insight into pollution. It involves no clear-cut distinction between sacred and secular. The same principle applies throughout. Furthermore, it involves no special distinction between primitives and moderns: we are all subject to the same rules. But in the primitive culture the rule of patterning works with greater force and more total comprehensiveness. With the moderns it applies to disjointed, separate areas of existence.
>
> (Douglas 1991 [1966]: 41)

Today's anthropologists would not talk about 'primitive' culture in this way. Instead they may refer to indigenous cultures as cultures trying to survive in the face of the juggernaut of capitalist modernisation. It is useful to think that the difference between the cosmologies of an overdeveloped multi-ethnic western country and a community struggling to maintain indigenous traditions is one of concentration. Today highly technologised metropolitan culture is dissipated and fractured, their cultural patterns and forms diffuse and scattered.

## THE VALUE AND LIMITS OF COSMOLOGY

To see the category dirt as operating as part of a cosmology that orders meaning and practice is a productive way of understanding culture. It is to see certain words and concepts as organising culture and going far beyond their literal meaning. In this dirt can be seen as part of a symbolic realm. And this has been a very powerful way of thinking about culture. In this sense culture isn't so much about *matter* as it is about *meaning*. Clifford Geertz, an important cultural anthropologist, wrote, 'the concept of culture I espouse [ … ] is essentially a semiotic one. Believing, with Max Weber, that man is an animal suspended in webs of significance he himself has spun, I take culture to be those webs, and the analysis of it to be therefore not an experimental science in search of law but an interpretative one in search of meaning' (Geertz 1973: 5). This is to see culture as 'soft', made up of signs, symbols, meanings and nuance. Yet if such a semiotics remains at the level of 'code' it doesn't get to what is crucial about culture, which is that it *gets under your skin*. Such signs are not codes that are out there, but living relations that are within our collective 'insides'.

In this an understanding of culture as made up of symbols needs to be accompanied by an understanding of how such a culture is materialised as a living practice. In this the cultural historian Stephen Greenblatt's understanding of culture is useful because it emphasises the way that sets of meanings are *driven* by material practices and that without these culture would be too *thin* to have any bite:

> The ensemble of beliefs and practices that form a given culture function as a pervasive technology of control, a set of limits within which social behavior must be contained, a repertoire of models to which individuals must conform. [ … ] The most effective disciplinary techniques practiced against those who stray beyond the limits of a given culture are probably not the spectacular punishments reserved for serious

offenders – exile, imprisonment in an insane asylum, penal servitude, or execution – but seemingly innocuous responses: a condescending smile, laughter poised between genial and sarcastic, a small dose of indulgent pity laced with contempt, cool silence. And we should add that a culture's boundaries are enforced more positively as well: through a system of rewards that range again from the spectacular (grand public honors, glittering prizes) to the apparently modest (a gaze of admiration, a respectful nod, a few words of gratitude).

(Greenblatt 1995: 225–26)

To be named and shamed as 'dirty' is to be subjected to those disciplinary techniques, to be refused glittering prizes. Greenblatt's sense of culture being enacted by a multitude of minuscule gestures and glances is important. Culture isn't all large symbols or emphatic rituals.

This became clear to the anthropologist Paul Rabinow when he was conducting fieldwork in Morocco in the 1960s. Trained in the social sciences at the University of Chicago, and well-versed in the structuralist anthropology of Claude Lévi-Strauss, Rabinow went to urban and rural Morocco in search of symbolism and ritualistic activities through which Moroccan culture could be interpreted and understood. But his reflections are aimed instead at the day-to-day activity of interacting with his 'informant' and friend Ali. Rabinow's reflections are about a frustration with the conventions of an anthropology that focuses on the symbolic and ritualistic and its lack of interest in the much less exotic world of humdrum everyday life. For Rabinow an argument with Ali reveals just how little he understands of Ali's day-to-day world – it is the nuance of everyday behaviour he doesn't get, while the cosmology of culture as it is embedded in symbols and rituals is relatively easy to comprehend:

Where a successful cultural form provides an ongoing framework for interpreting and generating experience, here the experience of the Other is most comprehensible. Boundaries are easily discernible, symbols are neatly situated, and sequence is explicitly controlled. It is here, not surprisingly, that anthropology has been most successful in describing and understanding other cultures. Yet it is in the less explicitly shaped and less overtly significant areas of day-to-day activity and common-sense reasoning that most cultural differences are embedded. Thematic observation is disturbingly difficult, for these phenomena are everywhere, thereby proving the most opaque to the methodologies we have developed. There are no clear boundaries to conclusively limit and define cultural performance. Ritual certainly has its complexities, but they are of a different order from those more scattered, fragmentary, and partial orderings which give coherence to social life.

(Rabinow 1977: 58)

The day-to-day activities of culture might be the most difficult for anthropology to see in their everydayness. In some ways it has been modernist *literary* ambitions that have attempted to capture the everydayness of the everyday. We can see this in books like Virginia Woolf's *Mrs Dalloway* or *Jacob's Room* (see Woolf 2012). But it is still an ambition for contemporary literature. The Norwegian writer Karl Ove Knausgaard, for instance, in his autobiographical novels detailing the minutiae of his ordinary life (the series is called *My Struggle* in English) could be seen as a contemporary example (see Knausgaard 2014).

In chapters 5 and 6 I make an argument that culture has been well-served in the past by forms of analysis that have managed to grasp its cosmologies. This is, inevitably, culture seen from a distance, and has been the version of culture that cultural studies has traded in. But culture as otherness, even as self-otherness, is a perspective that needs to be supplemented or countered by another view of culture, one that sees culture from the inside (even if in the process it sometimes can't quite see it as culture). This has been the province of literature, drama, films, songs, artworks and poems. In many ways the relationship between culture in its evaluative meaning the 'best which has been thought and said' and culture as an anthropological meaning needs to be rethought. On the one hand much of what goes by the name of culture in an anthropological sense is aimed at forms of improving (of producing better, cleaner subjects). On the other hand the culture of a 'selective tradition' *could* provide some of the best resources we have for offering ways of making sense of culture, of plotting trajectories through the internal logics of anthropologically inflected culture. There is a need, I think, to make a common cause between the study of culture as a complex whole and the sort of ambitious 'dirty' attempts that have fought their way through the complexity in the name of literature, art, popular culture, television and so on. There is a need to fashion new hybrid genres for the study of culture, ones that deploy a concern with descriptive writing as a way of getting a sense of culture as process, as *life*, as that life that is lived under the skin and on the skin. This genre is already in existence and it is the task of chapter 5 to show something of its productivity in the area of cultural studies. But before we get to that I need to turn to the topic of politics and what it might mean to think about a form of cultural politics.

# 4

## POLITICS

Both the term 'politics' and the term 'culture' can become all-encompassing. We have already seen in the last chapter how 'culture' can be seen as a realm which mediates *all* experience. Similarly an argument could be made that everything is, potentially at least, political. Conjoining the terms politics and culture, then, is not going to make the job of clarification any easier: if all is cultural, and all is potentially political, then the net that cultural politics can cast could be unfeasibly and unhelpfully large. So rather than add to the vagueness of the term it is necessary to work systematically and to ask questions about 'what is *cultural* about politics and what is *political* about culture' (Armitage, Bishop and Kellner 2005: 1).

In this chapter I am going to work to clarify what 'cultural politics' could be, in terms of the sorts of values and procedures that 'politics' could inflict on culture, and how it could direct the work of culture to particular ends. This doesn't mean that I espouse the subsuming of culture by politics, far from it. The point of this clarification is to be able to have more of a sense of the different kinds of work being done in the name of culture *and* politics so that there could be room for a number of approaches, some of which have determined political goals (to effect particular changes, or to work towards that goal) and some of which have analytic goals which may or may not have political effects, and some of which will clearly not have any political effects in the short term but may make the world more understandable, more open to description, or simply more vivid.

To this end I have two examples that I will look at in later sections. The first of these is the continual discussion over the use of headscarves and veils (the hijab and the burqa or niqab) by Muslim women in France and other secular or non-Muslim countries. The second relates to artists and writers who have been portraying the way that humans interact with the earth and the sea, and the way that the forces of capitalism and human endeavour are affecting the environment (what today is referred to as the Anthropocene). But before these examples I want to explore the imbrications of politics and culture by working from politics to culture and then back from culture to politics so that we can recognise points of similarity but also points of difference and points of conflict.

## FROM POLITICS TO CULTURE AND BACK AGAIN

Let's start by using a restricted example of the term politics: a political party or a political movement within parliamentary democracies. Here politics is the activity of trying to affect social change by garnering popular support for such change. The political movement could be environmentalism, it could be a proto-fascist nationalist party, it could be the 'radical centrist' position that many political parties try and inhabit today. The differences matter a great deal, of course, but all of them bring with them, in the name of politics, what they consider to be an *improvement* to life. In this there is a similarity between a restricted notion of politics and a restricted notion of culture (to cultivate, to improve). Each political party might have a number of quite specific policies or laws (lower taxation, laws against carbon emissions, changes in immigration protocols, and so on) that would clearly affect cultural life, in that large anthropological sense of the term culture. They might also have opinions about a more limited sense of culture (in terms of 'the best which has been thought and said') and this might inform policies about what should be taught in schools and how much of the national budget should be directed towards the arts.

In this sense a 'politics of culture' would point most immediately to areas of cultural policy at the level of government spending as well as a politicisation of areas of specific cultural activity. We see this all the time when, for example, a political party in government decides it wants to intervene in terms of the kind of history that gets taught in school or when it wants to prescribe the novels that should be read when a child is studying literature. We see this aspect of a politics of culture when a political party criticises a museum or a television channel for promoting what they consider to be an objectionable aspect of life. In the 1990s this aspect of a politics of culture became particularly prevalent in the United States when art exhibitions, which previously might have received a review in the cultural pages of a newspaper, became headlines, or were discussed in Washington.

Often the arguments that were directed against the art galleries were by political conservatives who argued that art was becoming *too* politicised, and by this they often meant that it was representing the lives of those who had been marginalised in society (for instance there was a good deal of furore over the work of the photographer Robert Mapplethorpe's work which pictured gay male sexuality). What were referred to at the time as the 'culture wars' was often an attack on *other* forms of cultural politics (a politics of culture directed at issues of 'race', feminism, environmentalism, sexuality, disability and so on, often referred to as identity politics). It was an attempt to claim for culture a particular morality that often spoke in the name of traditional values. As we have already seen it is not uncommon for conservatives to see culture as a political platform for quelling disquiet within a population; for instance General Pitt-Rivers (in chapter 2) thought that a presentation of material culture displayed as an evolutionary process could be used to ward off radical change. Culture, in a restricted sense of 'the arts' as a sense of national heritage, has always been useful for governments, as well as for the more general politics of capitalism (in some ways art is the archetypal commodity in that its exchange value dwarfs its use value).

In the midst of the Cold War, in the years following the Second World War, the United States put a good deal of energy into mounting vast exhibitions that toured the world and promoted the US as a liberal country that welcomed 'free expression'. Such strategies were aimed precisely *against* the cultural values that America perceived in the Soviet Union, which were figured by the United States as un-free by comparison. An exhibition like *The Family of Man*, which travelled the globe under a message of 'universal culture' (culture seen here as an anthropological realm), could similarly promote a 'neutral message' (we all die, cry, work, love) in an explicit attempt to further specific political interests (see Barthes 1973 [1957]: 100–102). Even an exhibition that was purportedly aimed at ameliorating political differences (the *American National Exhibition* in Moscow in 1959) would have been seen by many as exacerbating such differences (and seen like this at the time by all the parties involved):

> According to Harold C. McClellan, the general manager of the American National Exhibition, the exchange was meant to be a 'major step toward building better relationships and improved understanding between the United States and the Soviet Union'. This statement, however, told only part of the story. The exhibition was also a tool of cultural diplomacy against the Soviet Communist regime.
>
> (Kushner 2002: 6)

The idea of 'cultural diplomacy' is an instance where culture and politics come together in a peculiarly knotted way. An exhibition such as the *American National Exhibition* brought together the traditional fine arts alongside more experimental culture (in particular a multi-screen film by Charles and Ray Eames called *Glimpses of the USA*), as well as commodities (famously, examples of fancy hi-tech fitted-kitchens) in which the US displayed its commercial wealth. The Eames' film alone articulates two levels of culture: a presentation of an American 'way of life' (and the film concentrated on the most everyday aspects of US culture) declaring this is how we live, and an avant-garde film projected onto seven giant screens declaring that this is the sort of experimental work that is actively supported in the USA. At the exhibition, high culture, ethnographic culture and commodity culture (the best that has been bought and sold) are conjoined into a politics of 'soft power' (which is the power that culture wages and the euphemism that 'cultural diplomacy' names).

Of course cultural politics isn't necessarily aimed against a cultural foe. The example of the European Capitals of Culture programme is a case in point. It states its mission entirely in positive terms:

> The European Capitals of Culture initiative is designed to: highlight the richness and diversity of cultures in Europe; celebrate the cultural features Europeans share; increase European citizens' sense of belonging to a common cultural area; foster the contribution of culture to the development of cities. In addition to this, experience has shown that the event is an excellent opportunity for: regenerating cities; raising the international profile of cities; enhancing the image of cities in the eyes of their own inhabitants; breathing new life into a city's culture; boosting tourism.
>
> (EU Creative Europe website 2015)

Here the political use of culture (as we also saw in chapter 1 with the example of the UK City of Culture project) can be seen to be both cultural and economic: its aim is to celebrate and retrench a notion of identity (as European but also as a cultural identity within Europe) at the same time as it seeks to reap economic benefits through regeneration and tourism. This is culture (in the limited sense of art and heritage) deployed in quite specific ways. It follows in the wake of what urban geographers and journalists recognised as gentrification: namely that art and culture can be a prime agent in turning a down-at-heel neighbourhood into an up-and-coming one.

Such a cultural politics speaks in the name of democracy (art for everyone! everyone for art) but works on a pattern of investment that earmarks money for branding exercises that ensures that the long-term benefits do nothing to overcome the structural inequality within a city. It is perhaps no wonder that the monuments of creative culture of the Capitals of Culture are often met with indifference by people living in the city who might have quite a different idea of culture. One of the European Capitals of Culture in 2015 is the city of Mons in Belgium and like other cities who have taken on the title the emphasis has been on cultural branding:

> The whole European Capital of Culture endeavour breeds a relentlessly shallow logic, that a dose of metropolitan sparkle can be bought by importing a clutch of celebrity architects and their signature shapes. Like children drawing up a Christmas wish-list, it encourages mayors to dream big and lust after buildings they don't need and can't afford, too often leaving a slew of oversized, underused cultural monuments in its wake.
>
> Leaving Mons by train, I ask the city's press officer what the new station will eventually be like. 'Oh it's just the same as the Calatrava station in Liège,' she says, referring to the €300m rail hub that opened five years ago. 'Most people in Mons are much more excited about the imminent arrival of IKEA – it will be the first ever branch in Wallonia.'
>
> (Wainwright 2015)

If the citizens of Mons are more avidly awaiting IKEA than newly fashioned cultural monuments then the divergent aspects of culture could see this not as pitting 'cultural cognoscenti' against philistinism, but of describing two quite divergent ideas of culture as existing together. The political rationale for these capitals of culture might appear to be identity building, yet the underlying motive is more likely to be economic boosterism.

Culture and politics are embroiled even more thoroughly in forms of identity politics where the political project often seeks recognition of a particular 'cultural' experience as the basis for an improvement in community life. Thus an identity politics based on feminism and gender equality is premised on a requirement that sexism as an experience is recognised: as I mentioned in chapter 3, without the recognition of sexism it would be hard to see the political purpose of feminism. In terms of clarifying or describing the overlaps between politics and culture this requires an expansion of both the terms: what is being recognised is a form of experience that could be seen as endemic to the lived culture of a group. This is culture in its most anthropological form as a complex whole. Similarly it will require a politics that is expansive and goes much further than attempting to garner governmental power to create change: or rather the changes that are required go far beyond the role of legislature. There may, for instance, be laws in place that outlaw sexual discrimination in allocating pay or appointing jobs, but sexism exists at the level of the everyday, in the ubiquity of forms of talk, forms of behaviour, and forms of relationship. And these exist, to a large extent, beyond the rule of law (and certainly beyond the arm of law). Identity politics reveals to us that *all* of culture is to some degrees political, and all of culture can tip into an explicit political situation (for instance, the wearing of hijab headscarves). An ethnographic sense of culture does not describe a neutral world but a force field whereby certain practices are deemed legitimate and others are not, some are seen as normal and others are seen as deviant, or perverse, or subversive, or subservient.

Just as politics can be found everywhere within a broad understanding of culture as a 'whole way of life' it is also true that culture as a narrowly defined realm of 'the arts' can always be, to some degree, political. Writing in 1946 the journalist and novelist George Orwell explained why he was a writer. For him politics was his major impetus for writing:

> Using the word 'political' in the widest possible sense. Desire to push the world in a certain direction, to alter other peoples' idea of the kind of society that they should strive after. Once again, no book is genuinely free from political bias. The opinion that art should have nothing to do with politics is itself a political attitude.
>
> (Orwell 1946: 26)

As we have seen cultural conservatives (who are often also politically conservative) often pursue a form of politics based on the premise that culture is non-political, or should be non-political. In examples mentioned above, a Cold War anti-communist cultural position might claim that expressionist art isn't political at all, and this in itself becomes a political position and a political way of operating ('how can you consider this propaganda, it is an abstract painting, it is "beyond" politics, it is a sign of freedom, something that you in the Soviet Union don't have').

As cultural analysts we might want to recognise that all cultural texts require some form of explanation that links them to society and thereby links them to politics (in at least the most general sense of the term). A basic materialist assumption is that culture (as a whole way of life and the consciousness that goes with that) is a product of real material and historical circumstances. To try and explain a painting or a novel by recourse to ideas about individual genius is merely mystification. Cultural analysis (if it is to pursue a materialist approach) is required to explain how a work took the form that it did, how it articulated the themes that it did, and to show that this was 'determined', by a complexity of forces (which might include contingencies) that links it to a number of larger social and cultural 'frames' (the largest of which might be the changing role of art within society). In as much as we seek to explain culture (narrow or widely conceived) we will necessarily require social and political explanations of historical change.

In what follows I want to return to some of these points through two examples. The goal of these examples is not to provide a comprehensive cultural analysis of the topics being considered: there isn't the space for that, nor would it be appropriate for a book such as this. My examples are aimed at clarifying the relationship between culture and politics (which, to be fair, should really deserve a separate volume dedicated to the overlap) and to work towards a functional relationship of these terms so that they could be used to provide more precise forms of analysis beyond the vague sense that everything is cultural, everything is political.

## RELIGION, CULTURE, AND WOMEN-WHO-COVER

If you were to take a global survey of women's clothing you might come across some broad patterns that could connect clothing habits and choices to national and ethnic traditions, religious affiliation, wealth and class and age (you would not thereby exhaust the explanations of women's clothing, but I think it would be enough to point to some general patterns that connect a culture of clothing to wider social and political forces). One of the general patterns you might find is that in the wealthy Northern countries women reveal more bare flesh than in poorer Southern and Middle Eastern countries. This wouldn't be immediately understandable as an effect of climate, though there are good reasons for covering-up in the face of a ferocious sun. An explanation that looked to religion might have better luck. It is true that in what is called the Islamic world women tend to dress more modestly than they do in, say, Berlin. But does religion explain this? How do we then explain that in Christian Africa women dress modestly too?

We could then say that clothing is a pre-eminent cultural object: it contributes to cultural identity (national, ethnic, or group identity); it articulates ideas of propriety, sexuality, and aspiration; it demonstrates religious affiliations or the lack of them; and so on. Within a world of cultural differences for women to use clothing to cover their hair looks just like one choice amongst others. A marker of cultural difference. In recent years, especially after the September 11 2001 attacks in New York, clothing that is marked-out as Islamic has played a different role: no longer simply cultural, forms of headscarves have become political in quite precise ways. Indeed the plight of Afghan women was insistently offered in explanations as to why the United States and United Kingdom went into Afghanistan soon after September 11 (aside from dismantling al-Qaeda training camps). The 'humanitarian' mission was framed partly as liberating Afghan women from the Taliban who were insisting that they wear burqas (the full covering of the head and the body). Women's clothing, where it is connected to forms of Islamic observance in the Middle East and elsewhere, became symbolic of un-freedom.

Writing during the first wave of US–UK troop deployment in the region the anthropologist Lila Abu-Lughod titled an essay 'Do Muslim Women Really Need Saving?' In the essay she asks what the study of culture can contribute to the debates about women's lives under the Taliban in relation to a mission to fight the Taliban. One of the things she notices is that the association of covered clothing simply with oppression lacks any understanding of clothing traditions within Afghanistan or in the Middle East. The idea that Afghan women would be desperate to slip into jeans and a t-shirt once the Taliban had been thwarted was a colonial fantasy that refused to see how clothing is a part of deep culture. Abu-Lughod suggests that the sort of subtlety that people bring to their own clothing is necessary to understand clothing associated with Afghan women:

To draw some analogies, none of them perfect, why are we surprised that Afghan women do not throw off their burqas when we know perfectly well that it would not be appropriate to wear shorts to the opera? At the time these discussions of Afghan women's burqas were raging, a friend of mine was chided by her husband for suggesting she wanted to wear a pantsuit to a fancy wedding: 'You know you don't wear pants to a WASP [White-Anglo-Saxon-Protestant] wedding,' he reminded her. New Yorkers know that the beautifully coiffed Hasidic women, who look so fashionable next to their dour husbands in black coats and hats, are wearing wigs. This is because religious belief and community standards of propriety require covering the hair. They also alter boutique fashions to include high necks and long sleeves.

(Abu-Lughod 2002: 785)

We could say that to understand the politics of women's practices of covering their hair and sometimes covering their face as well means first of all treating it as cultural practice rather than a political one, and this might mean inquiring into its history, its geographical variations, and the meanings it has for Muslim women themselves.

If, from the perspective of a certain western ethnocentric view, covered women are seen as un-enlightened about women's liberation or about modernity, then a cultural perspective would have to plur-alise the perspectives on offer. How does the range of headscarves and coverings, for instance, alter from place to place, how might a modern hijab look in comparison to the burqa? For Abu-Lughod (and presumably for most Muslim women) dress that demon-strates Islamic observance is hugely varied and will have all sorts of meanings across the globe: 'the modern Islamic modest dress that many educated women across the Muslim world have taken on since the mid-1970s now both publicly marks piety and can be read as a sign of educated urban sophistication, a sort of modernity' (Abu-Lughod 2002: 786). The longer history of head-covering clothing in the Middle East has seen it associated less with reli-gious piety or with ethnic specificity and more with social status (Dwyer 2008: 142). It is also a form of clothing that is impossible for many to disassociate from the colonial histories that have surrounded it. Thus in the context of France, where the wearing of the hijab in public schools was made illegal as an 'ostentatious' act of wearing religious symbols (which also included the wearing of large crucifixes), forms of veiling connected to the longer history of France's colonial presence in the Maghreb region of North Africa and the Middle East have given Islamic clothing strong political resonances:

> The struggle over Maghrebin women's dress began long before their immigration to France in the 1970s. French and British colonizers encouraged Muslim women to remove the veil and emulate European women. Consequently, in Algeria and other North African and Middle Eastern countries, the veil became a symbol of national identity and opposition to the West during independence and nationalist movements.
>
> (Killian 2003: 570)

The same set of clothing practices, then, can have multiple significations: as a sign of women's oppression or 'backwardness' (for neo-colonialists in the west); as a sign of modernity; as a marker of religious observance; as a form of national identity; anti-colonialism; and so on.

Forms of veiling might always have had a political significance, but this is due to historical forces that have decided that Muslim women need saving. (The political significance of blue jeans is partly to do with its invisibility as a politicised form of clothing, yet seen with Afghan eyes it must sometimes look like the uniform of a huge group that has signed-up to a specific set of values.) In the French context any form of veiling in a public institution looks like a refusal to follow the principles of laicism of the French state which insists on the separation of the state and religion. For French legislation, as mentioned above, the wearing of a hijab is taken as an *ostentatious* religious symbol. For the girls who are wearing them, though, it might not be a symbol of anything at all, in the same way that habitual forms of clothing lose their symbolism for the wearer (in this sense blue jeans do not do symbolic work for their owners, at least most of the time). As one author, who had talked to a number of Maghrebian women after the 'headscarf affair' in France in 1989 (when three teenage girls were expelled from school in Creil after refusing to remove their headscarves), wrote, 'they do not view the veil as a symbol and, therefore, do not understand why girls wearing it in French class-rooms would be a problem' (Killian 2003: 575). In other words the *ostentation* is in the eyes of someone who has a very precise sense of what should be worn for the cultural probity of French public institutions. One woman of Moroccan descent saw the ban on wearing headscarves as specifically aimed at disrespecting, not religion but culture:

> I find that it's really an attitude on the part of teachers that is really racist, truly. That for me, is a racist act. We cannot exclude girls because they wear the headscarf ... It's really pointing a finger at them, and then vis-à-vis the culture of the child, they say to her 'your culture, it's no good.' You don't have a right to judge like that.
>
> (Killian 2003: 577)

But if there is an explicit cultural politics to covered clothing on a global stage that is animated more by the fantastical fear of ter-rorism than by terrorist acts, then there is also a more prosaic, everyday politics of clothing performed by teenagers negotiating a host of forces and demands in their lives. For British Muslim teenage girls the issue of what to wear is determined by fears of being racially bullied at school and in the street, of not wanting to dis-respect their parents and their shared cultural values, of wanting to embrace modern fashions and to be part of British culture, and, crucially, not wanting to simply mimic the clothing of an older generation. For many this meant having to come up with inventive solutions that allowed them to dress modestly, to dress fashionably, and to not be marked-out as ethnically distinct, as 'Asian':

> The *shalwar kameez* favoured by the older generation as appropriate 'Islamically-conformist' attire was replaced by some young women by long skirts and loose-fitting trousers. They saw these new dress styles as both more fashionable and also as fulfilling parental expectations about modest dress. Indeed they challenged their parents on these terms: 'They mix up religion and culture as well. Like it doesn't

say in the religion or anything, it just says that you've got to be covered, but the women don't see it like that. It's like you've got to wear Asian clothes.' 'It's like wearing a long skirt, wearing westernised clothes, which cover you up. They turn round and [say] you can't wear it because you're not allowed to wear it. And we say we're right because we're covering ourselves and there's nothing wrong with wearing it.'

(Dwyer 2008: 144)

In their negotiations with an older generation these young women prove to have an excellent command of the usefulness of separating the religious from the cultural and of arguing for a degree of openness to how a religious injunction is carried out.

The same distinctions should be made against the political symbolisation of Muslim clothing in debates about dress in culture more generally. To politicise headscarves and veils within the context of western cultures is to deploy an interpretative schema (of oppression, of 'backwardness', of 'ostentatiousness') on to cultural practices that are not for non-Muslims to interpret. The point of cultural analysis is not to interpret the world according to a set of principles that are fashioned in one cultural context and then apply it to another (this is what ethnocentrism is); rather it is to try and understand cultures from the inside so that differences can be accommodated not obliterated. If making a headscarf into a symbol of oppression is an ethnocentric form of politics, then is there another form of politics that could accompany a more empathetic cultural analysis? Such a politics would have to move away from the realm of symbolism and would need to work dialogically to allow the 'emergence of a new form of Muslim identity politics', one that 'highlighted questions about the ways in which cultural and religious differences might be accommodated, within dominant understandings of liberal democracy' and which might result in the recognition 'that Muslims had legitimate concerns relating to the fact that their religious needs were not always being met, the focus being on issues such as halal meat in schools and hospitals, provision for prayer at work or school, and accommodation of suitable dress for Muslim girls at school' (Dwyer 2008: 141). Such a form of cultural politics would recognise the different patterns of culture. The politics informing it would also require its own pattern, hopefully one patterned less on conflict and domination, and more on symbiosis and empathy.

## CULTURE AND CAPITALISM AND THE ANTHROPOCENE

In this section I want to look at a few cultural producers whose work has represented humankind's interaction with the environment, particularly around water. Obviously, in the space I have here I can't provide the sort of discussion that could do justice to the work. What I want to do instead is to explore what it might mean to investigate the world (and representations of that world) through the prism of cultural politics. What sort of questions should we ask *in the name* of 'cultural politics', and how might they be different from the sort of questions we can ask in the name of cultural values (for instance values associated with art) or in the name of politics (a politics whose primary concern would be the improvement of the social world)? In this brief investigation I will use the German critic Walter Benjamin as an aid to defining the terms of what might constitute 'cultural politics'.

The first artist I want to briefly consider is the Canadian photographer Edward Burtynsky. Burtynsky takes large format photographs with a plate-camera (which means that they have a sharpness and detail to them that you would not be able to achieve with smaller cameras). The camera also uses film stock (rather than digital data) to record – which also give immense detail and heightened verisimilitude. When he is taking photographs he looks like a figure from a previous era: he has to look through the ground glass screen of the camera with a black hood over his head so that he can see the image. When you look at his photographs in a museum or gallery you are faced with very large colour prints of enormous landscapes some of which have humans in them and some do not. They all confront you with the scale of humankind's actions on the earth. The landscapes that Burtynsky has photographed include copper mines in Montana and Utah, open-pit coal mines in British Columbia, nickel mining in Ontario, marble quarries in Italy, oil fields throughout Alberta and California,

*Figure 4.1* Edward Burtynsky, *Shipbreaking #27*, Chittagong, Bangladesh, 2000. © Edward Burtynsky, courtesy Nicholas Metivier Gallery, Toronto/Flowers, London.

shipbreaking in Chittagong, Bangladesh, and more recently urban expansion, dam building, and manufacturing industry throughout China.

The image I want to concentrate on is one from the Bangladesh *Shipbreaking* series. The images from the series show young Bangladeshis breaking up massive container ships on the beach. The work is very dangerous, many of the people working on the ships are still children, and it is (it almost goes without saying) badly paid work. Burtynsky describes the context of making the photographs:

> As part of my preparation I arranged for a fellow to hire a boat and run along the whole shore and photograph every ship that was being dismantled. I asked him to make me a map and draw a line where the sun comes up and where the sun goes down so I would know where

the ships were and how the sun was going to play on them. We also charted the tides.

And then I was standing there, standing on the beach with a view camera and a hood over my head and a group of five people helping me along. I'm sure the workers had never had a photographer like this in their midst. In that gaze across this space I was reminded in a way of nineteenth-century exploration, standing, looking at a culture revealing itself to you.

(Burtynsky interviewed in Pauli 2003: 54)

He is clearly aware of the uneven power relations that exist in this context, and has the historical knowledge to be aware that he may well be rehearsing a form of colonial encounter. He is also clear about the sort of cultural values that are important to him: a certain kind of light, a certain ratio of land and water.

As a viewer confronted with these images in an art gallery (which is where they are exhibited) you are faced with extremely large photographs that have a sharpness of detail that is uncanny. The dominant colours of the earth take on the same tones as the rusted metal. In philosophical aesthetics the term 'sublime' is used to refer to views that go beyond beauty and include something daunting, frightening or humbling. This is often the result of scale: the sublime belittles the human body through its size, or through its grandeur. The skeletons of container ships become behemoths beached in Bangladesh – a technological sublime, somehow naturalised through age and decrepitude. In some sense the images seem to belong to Matthew Arnold's search for 'sweetness and light', if it wasn't for the grim and dangerous subject matter. It is hard not to view such work as beautiful or sublime, and a viewer can find themselves muttering 'oohs' and 'ahs' as they wander round an exhibition of his work.

The cultural (in the sense of the arts and aesthetic pleasure) takes precedence over the political even if the political is embedded in the image. The relationship of culture and politics is something that Burtynsky has obviously considered:

There are times when I have thought about my work and putting it into a more politicized environment. If I said this is a terrible thing you are doing to the planet, then people will either agree or disagree. By not saying what you should see, that may allow them to look at something that they had never looked at and to see their world a little differently.

(Burtynsky talking in the film *Manufactured Landscapes*)

It is a considered position, and the viewers of his work often face a deeply affective contradiction between the intense visual pleasure of the photographic image (as saturated with rich colour, as a field of endless detail) and the substantive content of the image which is always of environmental damage. Such a contradiction makes for a memorable experience and Burtynsky's images, seen in the flesh so to say, stay with you. And yet does it constitute a cultural *politics* and if so what sort of a politics is it?

Here the words of Walter Benjamin might clarify Burtynsky's work. In 1934 Benjamin wrote an essay (which was presented as a lecture) titled 'The Author as Producer' which outlines a form of cultural politics. For Benjamin a cultural politics could not be contained within the choice of subject matter nor could it be contained within the individual artwork: 'the rigid, isolated object (works, novel, book) is no use whatsoever. It must be inserted into the context of living social relations' (Benjamin 1934: 87). Thus, for Benjamin, the political side of cultural politics required thinking about the relationships between author and subject matter, author and viewer, and author and technology. In this essay Benjamin was scathing about what he saw as a tendency for photographers to tackle political subject matter in a particular way: '[photography] has become more and more subtle, more and more modern, and the result is that it is now incapable of photographing a tenement or a rubbish-heap without transfiguring it. [ ... ] It has succeeded in turning abject poverty itself, by handling it in a modish, technically perfect way, into an object of enjoyment' (Benjamin 1934: 94–95). It is hard not to see Burtynsky's work in this way: it is beautiful. What we don't have any sense of is the social context of the labour that is being performed on this beach in Chittagong. Seen through a prism of culture Burtynsky's work offers an affective contradiction between beautiful formal values and abhorrent social content. Seen through a prism of cultural politics he offers a sensational experience to gallery goers who are not given the materials to translate this experience into something that reaches beyond the gallery.

The second example is a recent film from the US called *Leviathan* (2012) (not to be confused with a Russian film with the same name that came out in 2014 by the director Andrey Zvyagintsev). The *Leviathan* that I'm interested in was directed by two anthropologists, Lucien Castaing-Taylor and Verena Paravel, working with the Sensory Ethnographic Laboratory (which Castaing-Taylor is the director of) at Harvard University. There is no reason to assume that Castaing-Taylor and Paravel want their documentary film to be seen within the context of cultural politics – yet responding to it within the terms of cultural politics could usefully elucidate one of the central aspects of the film.

Castaing-Taylor and Paravel filmed *Leviathan* on an industrial trawler operating off the coast of New Bedford, Massachusetts. It isn't your usual documentary. There is no voice-over narrative telling you about what you are seeing. The fishing crew are mostly silent, and when they do speak it isn't to tell us, the audience, how they feel or what they are thinking about the work, they are just talking to each other. But it is the way that it is

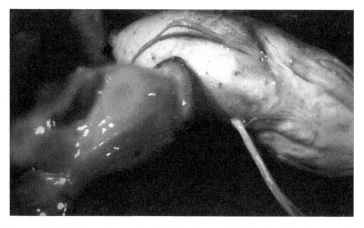

*Figure 4.2* Still from *Leviathan* (2012), directed by Lucien Castaing-Taylor and Verena Paravel.

filmed that is most striking. Castaing-Taylor and Paravel used a battery of waterproof cameras and attached them to the animate and inanimate 'workings' of the trawler. Cameras are attached to the anchor as it is cast into the black emptiness of the North Atlantic Ocean at night. A camera sloshes around with fish heads in a huge plastic trough. The effects are dizzying and pulverising. The cameras can't help but follow the roll, pitch and yaw of the vessel; the cameras linger on the labour and continue much longer than is needed to get the information of what the crew are doing; blood and guts, water and knives are not held at a distance but are drawn into the field of the camera. And it is clear that the directors are offering a different kind of knowledge about industrial fishing, one that offers a sensation of trawler life, where you are immersed in the material labour of fishing.

Of course *Leviathan* is a film and so it is offering us a mediated relationship to the labour of this fishing crew. But by altering the techniques of filming that mediation is different, its concerns are different and its affects are too. It is a film of sensations, it is vertiginous and it is repetitive to the point of agitated boredom. We stay with the fish heads for 'too long' (much longer than the conventions of narrative cinema would allow). We begin to squirm, get restless, we want something to 'happen'. Of course anyone who has done any factory work knows this experience all too well. This is what happens at the factory bench: time drags, your body tenses up, your muscles fidget, they have little flights of panic. The film might not be pitched as a form of cultural politics, yet in its dedication to offering sensory insights it certainly differs from the photography of Burtynsky. But does it satisfy Benjamin's notion of cultural politics? In his essay 'A Small History of Photography' Benjamin quotes the playwright Bertolt Brecht recognising the difficulty of simply showing reality:

> The situation is complicated by the fact that less than ever does the mere reflection of reality reveal anything about reality. A photograph of the Krupp works [a manufacturer of armaments] or the A.E.G. [a manufacturer of domestic appliances] tells us next to nothing about these institutions. Actual reality has slipped into the functional.

The reification of human relations – the factory, say – means that they are no longer explicit.

(Brecht cited in Benjamin 1931: 255)

*Leviathan* certainly goes some way beyond 'the mere reflection of reality' as a form of distancing. What we get instead is a visceral engagement with this reality that is the result of an inventive intervention into the situation, including looking at the work of trawlers from the perspective of dead fish and the mechanisms of the ship. Where its cultural politics may fall short is the relationship it articulates between the trawler, the crew and the larger social world of global trade, ocean husbandry, and so on.

The next two examples are both informed by Walter Benjamin's work on cultural politics and deliberately employ a range of aesthetic, discursive strategies to produce their work. Allan Sekula's *Fish Story* was a long-term project (Sekula died in 2013) that involved photographing shipyards and ships from across the world (from the US to Holland, from Cuba to Poland) and trying to understand the global industry that went with it. The undertaking was huge and involved Sekula travelling on container ships and

*Figure 4.3* Still from *The Forgotten Space* (2010), a film essay by Allan Sekula and Noël Burch.

talking to crews that undertake such work. It meant travelling to the Hyundai shipyards in Ulsan, South Korea to see container ships being built and the living conditions of those who are building the ships. The result was an exhibition and a book (*Fish Story*) and, later, a couple of years before he died, a film essay with Noël Burch called *The Forgotten Space*.

The book is made up of a range of registers: narratives of sailors and ports; photographs of derelict shipyards; historical accounts of shipbuilding and fishing; analysis of the culture of shipping and fishing; a history of the political economy of shipping and so on. The stories, images and analysis throw you into a tangled world of interconnections. To see a ship is to see a world of global trade that is hidden within the ship and needs to be drawn out:

> Things are more confused now. A scratchy recording of the Norwegian national anthem blares out from a loudspeaker at the Sailors' Church on the bluff above the channel. The container ship being greeted flies a Bahamian flag of convenience. It was built by Koreans labouring long hours in the giant shipyards of Ulsan. The crew, underpaid and over-worked, could be Honduran or Filipino. Only the captain hears a familiar melody.
>
> (Sekula 2002 [1995]: 12)

A ship that is viewed needs a narrative to accompany it. It needs a place of destination, an account of who built it, an understanding of its crew members, of the relationship between crew and company, and so on. Photographs demand more photographs, writing requires more writing. A conversation with a sailor requires a conversation with a welder, which might mean visiting someone's home. Such an undertaking requires an involvement with the social world of shipping that isn't necessarily on the level of sensual entanglement that is demonstrated by *Leviathan* but also goes further in mapping the geography of the sea as industry, as labour. As a sensual form *Fish Story* lacks the intensity of *Leviathan* and it clearly avoids the sublime aesthetics of Burtynsky, yet in terms of its politics it is clearly much more thoroughly involved in a social and political understanding of the culture of shipping. It is also much more engaged with thinking through the political *form* of photography and writing as a cultural practice:

> *A writer who does not teach other writers teaches nobody.* The crucial point, therefore, is that a writer's production must have the character of a model: it must be able to instruct other writers in the production and, secondly, it must be able to place an improved apparatus at their disposal. This apparatus will be the better, the more consumers it brings in contact with the production process – in short, the more readers or spectators it turns into collaborators.
>
> (Benjamin 1934: 98 italics in the original)

With *Fish Story*, Sekula provides a model for working that could be used by you or me (if we had the tenacity, the rigour and the resources) as a way of doing cultural work at a political level. To be clear, if this was *just* a question of politics then it wouldn't require what are quite complex forms. Working politically might

*Figure 4.4* Carole Condé and Karl Beveridge, *The Fall of Water*, 2007. © Carole Condé and Karl Beveridge, courtesy of the artists.

involve working with unions or with environmental campaigners on effecting change. Working within a cultural politics – one dedicated to Benjamin's ideas of transforming the cultural forms that you are working with in political ways – means that a politics is not simply an outcome, it is also a relationship with viewers, institutions and subjects.

My final example is Carole Condé and Karl Beveridge's photographic reworking of the painting *The Fall of the Rebel Angels* by Pieter Bruegel the Elder. Bruegel's painting is used as a template for Condé and Beveridge's figuring of a politics of water seen on a global level. Just like the medieval painting the photograph requires reading rather than just viewing. And to this end it comes with its own interpretative key:

> Characters representing the global breadth of water politics have replaced the Archangels in the Bruegel painting. In the middle, replacing Saint Michael, is an Andean indigenous woman representing the successful fight against water privatization in Cochabamba, Bolivia. On the left side is a South Asian woman representing the successful fight against the damming of the Narmada River in India. On the right is a Canadian environmentalist defending Canada's vast water resources. Activists of various nationalities and cultures have replaced the remaining eight angels. The abusers and the results of environmental abuse cover the ground: oil companies, industrial polluters, water bottlers, dam builders, privateers, agribusiness types, the military, corporate thieves, dead fish, oil-covered birds, drought, disease, E. coli, politicians, scientists, and the occasional unsuspecting victim floating among them.
>
> (Barber 2008: 71)

Such a work is again different from the other three examples. What we could say about the work is that it figures a global politics of water in a single complex image as a set of relations between various actors (multinationals, activist groups, natural resources and so on). Of course it doesn't explain how these things work or the history of their relationship. It does offer an image to identify with and a cultural form that could be used to different ends. In some ways one of the key things it does is suggest that medieval art, with its complex cosmologies, can be repurposed for different ends, and that art isn't necessarily about the spectacular, but about complex orchestrations.

In an essay concerned with the representational politics of photographers like Edward Burtynsky, Imre Szeman and Maria Whiteman continue the critique of Walter Benjamin, suggesting that a politics of representation will need to use a number of representational devices to render the Anthropocene of capitalism both intelligible *and* challengeable:

> The critical capacity of photography does not lie where one often imagines it to be – in either the mode of exposé (a journalistic imperative) or insight gained through an aesthetic trauma induced in the viewer (the avant-garde dream once again). It comes instead out of affirmation of what we might hope to hide, deny or reject. Stock markets and Chinese factories are blown up to gigantic proportions so that we might confront them, but also so that in confronting them we might wish them away. This is a politics of denial: the idea that the way to go forward is through laments about the wrong turnings we have already taken. But seen from another vantage point, photography's core indexicality constitutes a demand that we face up to the world as it is and deploy whatever representational means necessary to try to reframe our comprehension of it, in part and in whole, and in a manner that produces different landscapes for those image-makers to come.
>
> (Szeman and Whiteman 2009: 555)

In thinking about this we should not expect to find a single form for undertaking cultural politics: there is no perfect vehicle here. Condé and Beveridge's work is clearly totally different from Sekula's, but both could be seen to be invoking a complex whole as the material out of which to make culture. And both, but perhaps especially Condé and Beveridge's, emphasise the fact that these relationships are changeable and that a cultural politics might insist that we take sides, that we side with the Andean woman against the incursion of multinationals.

The point of this brief review of a number of cultural projects isn't to insist that culture (as a representational practice) should always be political, or that it should have to live up to the exacting standards of Walter Benjamin (though it would be nice if more cultural practices had that as their ambition). Lots of culture doesn't clearly want or need to have that relationship explicitly (though it is worth remembering that it is a conservative cultural politics that insists on arts' role as being non-political). Rather it is a way of clarifying the sorts of questions that are worth asking under the banner of cultural politics (a cultural politics of the left) and what questions would not be relevant. It is not enough for cultural politics to claim that subject matter alone makes for a progressive cultural politics as if another picture of the globally impoverished would do anything to the way the world is run or to our understanding of how the world is run. So the sorts of questions that we could ask of work that rides under the banner of cultural politics might be: does it offer a complex understanding of the world? Does it mobilise critical forces and does it galvanise people with a sense of where solutions might be found? Does it seek to explain how the world is how it is? Does it seek to offer a way forward? Does it provide new forms for continuing such work, does it offer models for the future?

A cultural politics might have to navigate some particularly difficult contradictions, for instance the ability to show the complex whole and to be popular at the same time. Cultural politics is perhaps the most difficult terrain to investigate. It is certainly a difficult field to inhabit. Perhaps the most useful advice to anyone combining the terms politics and culture is to give up on the search for purity, for absolutes.

# 5

## EXPERIENCE

Experience, as Mary Douglas argued (in chapter 3 above), is mediated by culture: we experience the world *through* culture; through its categories, forms, exemplifications and traditions. To understand experience from a cultural perspective requires charting the *patterns* of meanings and force within which experience takes place. As the anthropologist Edward Bruner put it: 'there are no raw encounters or naive experiences since persons, including ethnographers, always enter society in the middle. At any given time there are prior texts and expressive conventions, and they are always in flux' (Bruner 1986: 12). But the reason why these conventions don't simply freeze in a static feedback loop whereby experience and convention simply agree, is because our experiences are alive, changeable and, to some degree at least, are running ahead of convention. Experience, then, is not just the confirmation of cultural patterns it is also its most profound test.

The forms of representation that we have, and which constitute culture as a limited field (popular culture, journalism, the arts and so on), offer patterns of meaning but they do not exhaust the cultural field as a heterogeneous ensemble of experience:

> Society is a battlefield of representations, on which the limits and coherence of any given set are constantly being fought for and regularly spoilt. Thus it makes sense to say that representations are continually subject to the test of a reality more basic than themselves – the test of social practice. Social practice *is* that complexity which always outruns the constraints of a given discourse; it is the overlap and interference of representations; it is their rearrangements in use; it is the test which consolidates and disintegrates our categories, which makes or unmakes a concept [ ... ].
>
> (Clark 1985: 6)

In this sense the dynamics of the world of representation are both shaping experience as well as being tested (and often found wanting) by the world of experience.

Experience shares its etymological roots with *experiment*. At times culture does not completely tally with our on-going experience, something does not sit quite right, the categories do not quite fall into place. Experience is the test of cultural conventions, the test of their efficacy, of their adequacy. Experience also allows us to reimagine the disjuncture between culture as a limited and selected field of representations (of the best which has been thought and said) and culture as that extended anthropological realm that is all-encompassing. My argument is that we need mobile, inventive and reliable experiential maps if we are to make sense of our dynamic engagements and entanglements with culture. Indeed if cultural analysis works to connect the singularity of a lived experience to the larger social and cultural world that it is embedded in, then we would need fulsome accounts of living experience as well as useful accounts of that larger social and cultural world. We would need to select our guidebooks with care.

In this chapter, then, I am going to rehearse one of my core arguments for how we can negotiate through the vagaries of culture and the various conflicts its meanings pose. In the first section I'm going to detail that argument for you, going back over some of the ground we have already tracked. But I want to move on to look at the kinds of mobile and inventive maps that are already there for thinking and registering experience and for representing culture as a dynamic field. Some of these are part of a canon of works that might be taught in a literature class, some of them exist on the margins of disciplines like cultural studies, anthropology or sociology, others are found in examples of life-writing and auto-biography. The chapter ends with a defence of cultural aesthetics as a form of cultural analysis, that doesn't simply sit *within* culture as a symptom, nor *outside* it as a diagnosis of an exotic form. It sits across culture, attentive to the way that culture is lived at the level of *sensation* and *detail*, within a system that always exceeds this living but which can only be grasped in a network of experiences.

## AN ARGUMENT FOR REIMAGINING CULTURE

Matthew Arnold's argument that culture is the quest for perfection (a demand for what he called 'sweetness and light', a phrase that sounds particularly twee today) can be seen as part of an activity aimed at decreeing what is good and what is not, what is worthy of attention and what can and should be ignored. For many this is culture with a capital C, High Culture. It is to discriminate in the name of civility and civilisation. It is part of an effort to canonise certain works as 'the best'; to establish a tradition of works that could be used to call into being not just a select body of ideas, beliefs and manners, but a national culture. This is where the restricted version of culture is used as an ideological flag for a much more enlarged sense of culture (India as represented by Tagore; Chile as represented by Neruda; Britain represented by Shakespeare, and so on). Such a version of culture is rightly cri-ticised by pointing out that it represents only a particular version of a nation, and obscures as much as it brings to light. It was critiqued most effectively by Raymond Williams as a body of work that goes by the name of 'tradition' but must be seen as a *selective tradition*:

> For tradition is in practice the most evident expression of the domi-
> nant and hegemonic pressures and limits. It is always more than an
> inert historicized segment; indeed it is the most powerful practical
> means of incorporation. What we have to see is not just 'a tradition'
> but a *selective tradition*: an intentionally selective version of a shaping

past and a pre-shaped present, which is then powerfully operative in
the process of social and cultural definition and identification.

(Williams 1977: 115)

A selective tradition is there as a pre-selected set of great works:
great works of architecture, works of literature, great musical
achievements, a canon of great paintings and great thought, and
so on. It is what you learn in school. There are contradictions within
such a tradition of course. We should note that while a selective
tradition might operate to promote a national culture it can do so
by selecting works that are highly critical of the nation in question
and highly critical of nationalism as such. More important than
the actual items that make up the selective tradition of culture
(the best which has been thought and said) is the attitude that is
inculcated towards the selection. One such dominant attitude would
be that the tradition is made up of the works of great artists, and
creators, and that as recipients of this tradition all we need to do
is recognise these individual geniuses.

It is in this way that the selective tradition is precisely the reverse
of what Benjamin wanted from a cultural politics: it is the work of
art on its own, as a finished and complete edifice, removed from
labour, process and collectivity. Thus the selective tradition (as both
a selection and an attitude towards that selection) is the embodiment
of what Marx and Engels saw as the entanglement of consciousness
and class domination:

The ideas of the ruling class are in every epoch the ruling ideas, i.e. the
class which is the ruling material force of society, is at the same time
its ruling intellectual force. The class which has the means of material
production at its disposal, has control at the same time over the means of
mental production, so that thereby, generally speaking, the ideas of those
who lack the means of mental production are subject to it. The ruling ideas
are nothing more than the ideal expression of the dominant material
relationships, the dominant material relationships grasped as ideas.

(Marx and Engels 1970 [1846]: 64)

We would rightly, then, be highly suspicious of anyone who
would use the term 'culture' to signify a body of work whose

value is unquestionable, who uses culture to decide what should and should not count as important or worthwhile.

But does this mean that we have to refuse selectivity? Could we even if we wanted to? We might, for instance, need selectivity to challenge the selections that go to make up the canon of the selective tradition. We might want to argue that the lack of women within this tradition is appalling, and because of this we need to find ways of selecting women producers as a counter selection. We might want to argue that the immediate privileging of 'prestige culture' over ordinary culture (opera over musicals, say, or theatre over film) is unwarranted, and we might want to select a number of examples of films and musicals to make our point. But this is to stay within the logic of a selective tradition of canonical work, and the gradual addition of new forms as well as new works is very much part of that logic.

What happens when we want to include all forms of representational work under the banner of culture? And what happens when we decide to make culture that vast terrain signalled as 'a whole way of life' or as a 'complex whole'? Are we free from selectivity? First it should be pointed out that any attempt to figure a field, even as vast a field as the anthropological definition of culture, involves selection. Take, for example, the field of popular culture. One way of grasping this field is to talk about popular *genres* and *forms*. We might point to horror films, or soap operas, or romantic comedies as significant forms within the field. Already we are involved in categories, in taxonomies, that mean that while we incorporate a vast trove of material we select the categories for understanding them, for attending to them. But selection doesn't end there. In categorising genres we establish a set of values and conventions that one genre performs and another genre does not. Within any genre we have works that are seen to be exemplary of those conventions and values – they typify the genre, or they mark the moment when a certain convention was first deployed. Thus if we were looking at horror films as a genre within popular culture we would at some point come across *Night of the Living Dead* (1968, directed by George A. Romero) as a significant film within that genre, and one that established a new sub-genre of zombie films.

But what happens if we embrace the anthropological version of culture and suggest that it is basically the general practice of social life, that includes everything from eating to praying, everything from small talk to operatic arias? Selection might be a necessity simply because this is such an unmanageably vast terrain. But just as there is no naïve experience, there is no naïve selection: we come to the world already prepared to find some things more significant than others. And as cultural analysts informed by a *selective tradition* of cultural analyses we are already sensitised to select certain cultural practices over others, or to view cultural practices with particular attitudes. In this book, for instance, while I have been eager to treat culture as lived social practices I have had to select certain materials. More importantly, though, the attitudes I have put forward, for instance treating culture as a *pattern* rather than as a progression, is itself a form of selectivity. Indeed you only need to flip to the bibliography to see that this book enacts a selective tradition made up of proper names such as Ruth Benedict, Mary Douglas and Raymond Williams. So if we are always going to be involved in selecting it is worth thinking about what values we would want to employ in the business of selecting and how that selection will help us to make sense of the world. Do we want to keep Benedict and Williams as our guides to the field of culture? Shouldn't we consider instead theorists such as Michel Foucault and Pierre Bourdieu who might have important things to say about culture? What is it that we want from our selective tradition?

The distinction between culture 'as the best which has been thought and said' and culture as social practice is replicated at the level of cultural analysis but instead of the 'best' being poems and cantatas, it is the work of people such as Benedict, Williams, Foucault and Bourdieu. This is our selective tradition within academic studies of culture. If the relationship between a limited and selective tradition and social practice is in some sense inevitable then we might want to ask how we want this relationship to play out and if there are other ways of figuring the relationship. I want to suggest two ways of recasting this relationship and rethinking how we might go about the business of selection.

The first is that the current academic tradition of selectivity tends to reverse an earlier distinction between culture as limited and culture as expansive. Today our selection of the 'best which has been thought and said' tends towards the work of figuring 'culture at a distance'. To see culture as a pattern requires comparative perspectives, distant viewing, and theories of social structuring. A grand tradition of certain critical proper names (Marx, Freud, de Beauvoir, Fanon, Spivak, Jameson and so on) today might be as secure within the bastions of humanities and social science scholarship as proper names such as Shakespeare or Henry James, and a good deal more secure than names such as Elgar, Tagore and Plath. This theoretical tradition provides a perspective that often seeks to see culture as 'other' even if it is the host culture that is being viewed. This is the distant view, the view from the other shore. A previous canon of 'the best which has been thought and said' might well have included specific plays and bodies of thought (the 'classics'). Such work might have had less interest in the work of cultural patterning and the relativism that went with it. Such work (however skewed to dominant structures of power) might have been speaking from within culture. This is culture up-close and personal. The literary form of the novel, which became a privileged genre within this tradition, was seen by influential critics such as F. R. Leavis as a form that was informed by experience, and could offer us a privileged entry into experience. Otherwise why bother studying them? I certainly would not want to return to a situation where everyone has to study the same canon of the great tradition, but when I look around at university curricula I often think that we are doing precisely that, but now our canon is made up of 'great works of social and cultural theory'. If a canon is somehow inevitable, it should be dynamic, changeable, and available for restructuring.

The second way that we need to rethink this relationship is to think about scale. The selective tradition often included work that rendered culture on a small, intimate scale. Certainly the sort of novels that were highly valued within an English literary tradition were often of culture in the close. Jane Austen's novels talked about class and about gender and about historical change, but they did so at an intimate distance. This was culture from the inside. The critical theoretical tradition, however, views culture at a distance. It is culture from the outside. This relationship is perhaps extended today in academic versions of cultural studies and social sciences, whereby culture from the outside is given authority, canonicity and stability, and it is seen as the lens with which to view culture from the inside. But now culture from the inside is no longer a Jane Austen novel, but the world of the shopping mall, or the football terrace, or the biochemical lab. Experience, it would seem, is untrustworthy and would require the sorts of interpretative schemas that a canon of theoretical texts provides.

But what do we want from cultural analysis? Is our goal really to get a better reading of a soap opera or a better interpretation of a football chant? Do we want to know the precise language of subcultures? Of course we might certainly want such things but are they a goal to work towards or a means of getting to somewhere else? Isn't the ambition that is located in the expansiveness of the word culture an ambition to understand the totality, the complex whole? If we continue to work with our current canon of critical texts we will find the same totality time and again wherever we look because such a totality is already written in these texts. But actually if our job is to try and find the emerging totality then what we need is more culture from the inside with which to reimagine the totality. As far as this goes the division between culture as texts (and text-like objects) *requiring* interpretation and forms of critical theory that can *perform* the task of interpreting needs to be overcome. It is unhelpful. What is required is a different sense of scale within cultural analysis, a different emphasis on perspective and a different relationship between the singularity of cultural experience and the totality of the socio-cultural within which such experience exists.

What we need are a constantly changing canon of maps that are small scale and large scale and don't privilege one over the other. Such maps might have to move from the anecdotal to the systematic, from the microscopic to the macro view. We need to see totality as something not to inherit off the shelf from a selective tradition of social and cultural theory, but as forms to uncover and speculate about. We could then put a current tradition of figuring the totality under pressure by challenging it with a multitude of experiential moments. Thus an evaluative sense of culture could be envisaged that included 'the best' (for now) models for apprehending experience (culture in the unrestricted sense) and maps for rendering the field of culture. The totality of culture would not be found in readily available patterns that were known in advance nor would it be knowable as an endless collection of details. Instead it would be found *within* the multitude of instances through which it can be grasped. This means that analysis would work at a level of multiple singularities, seen as close-up experience, which would be positioned with larger and larger fields into which such experience is embedded. This isn't scientific work in the rationalist sense of this term. It is inventive work. It requires creative effort in describing lived particularity, of connecting particulars to each other, and of sketching-in the larger totality that might illuminate such experience and make it sing. We do not need a theoretical *system* to work with culture at this level; what we need are experiential maps that work at the level of the singularity of culture; that put emphasis on description and on detailing their singularity. Through such work we might imagine a totality of such singularities. This means *not* working at the level of the 'typical' (because the 'typical' means already assuming that there is a type that the typical fits), it means working with singularity – as if every experience, every subject is eccentric, but that it is in the eccentricity that the social is to be found.

## EXPERIENTIAL MAPS

In the early 1960s the novelist Georges Perec wrote an important essay titled 'For a Realist Literature'. Fundamentally, for Perec, the artwork, by offering an orchestration of the world, provides a coherent depiction:

> What we call an artwork isn't just the rootless creation that the aestheticist work is; on the contrary, it is the most total expression of concrete realities; if literature is a work of art, it is because it organizes and unmasks the world, because it makes the world appear in its coherence beyond its everyday anarchy, while integrating and surpassing the contingencies that render it in the form of the immediate system, with its necessity and its movement.
>
> (Perec 2007 [1962]: 32)

This is probably as good a description as you are going to get of a form of cultural analysis working within the tradition of Ruth Benedict's search for cultural patterns. Cultural analysis is in many ways an attempt to render chaos as coherence. It might sometimes overstep the mark in this by forcing culture into patterns of its own devising. Sometimes it is the anarchy of the everyday, the chaos of the social that *is* the pattern (the non-patterned pattern, so to say). The methodological basis of Perec's position is a dialectical movement between the general and the particular:

> Because the particular only appears as a function of the general, and because the general can only be grasped as a function of the particular, this self-conscious effort [to write in order to know oneself] that remains a point of departure for all creation (literary or not) can only be a point of departure, and remains useless if it doesn't integrate itself into a larger project involving reality in its entirety.
>
> (Perec 2007 [1962]: 33)

For Perec, then, realism is the struggle against the formlessness of 'everyday anarchy'. Its role is to find the general in the particular through the seemingly tautological route of recognising that the general can only function in its particularities.

Today it is not unusual to find the more experimental end of cultural analysis invoking literary writers such as Georges Perec or Marcel Proust as influences and guides for a certain form of descriptive ethnography. The sociologist Howard Becker suggests that Perec's early novel, *Things*, operates in an ethnographic manner to provide:

> An atmosphere more than a narrative, an aura that surrounds you rather than a journey you make. In this it strongly resembles an ethnographic description of a culture or a way of life, of shared understandings and routine activities undertaken in accord with them. It is just what an ethnography would give us. And Perec's ethnography is complete covering material culture, kinship and other social relations, work and technology, beliefs and values, typical careers and lives, and

all the other things ethnographers are enjoined to include in a 'complete' description of a culture.

(Becker 2001: 65–66)

I would agree with this analysis and yet the 'typicality' of the couple that Perec describes in his novel is not some sort of aggregate of the sorts of lives someone in this specific class and culture lives: rather it is by pursuing the singularity of a couple, their likes and dislikes, their failures and their phobias, that these lives are described. Perec's work suggests that there isn't just culture out there to be gathered up and analysed. The act of gathering together phenomena that go by the name of culture is itself the production of culture and is a way of bringing to consciousness inchoate experiences. It is an imaginative act of grasping the emergent, of fashioning culture in its becoming, rather than as what it became.

A more literary form of cultural analysis could mean that there are other ways of going about registering the cultural that don't require insisting on distance and the transformation of culture into an analytic object. A more literary form of cultural analysis might provide more empathetic experiential maps. In the recent interest in 'affect' (the term names what used to be called the passions – the emotional energies that exist socially and are felt as mood, emotion, attention and optimism [or the lack of it]) a number of writers involved in feminism and queer studies, across the social sciences and the humanities have pursued a more literary approach to cultural analysis. The presence of diary writing is one aspect of this, as is a substantial emphasis on description. This isn't 'fictional writing': its goal is to describe the social world of culture as it exists (which might actually be the goal of writing that goes by the name of 'fiction' too).

One example of the new experiential maps that are being produced of culture is Ann Cvetkovich's *Depression: A Public Feeling*. The first third of the book contains 'The Depression Journals' and is a 'memoir'. In this section Cvetkovich describes her bouts of depression and what sort of experience it was and is. She describes how her depression was caught up in all sorts of social worlds to do with academic achievement, to do with gender and sexuality and to do with the social world of North American life. The rest of the book constitutes 'a speculative essay' on public feeling and weaves together art projects, medical critiques and social criticism. In reading the book you realise that you can't separate the 'memoir' from 'the speculative essay', the one requires the other. They are both necessary mappings of culture seen through the perspective of a feeling made public and a feeling of the public. For Cvetkovich 'new conceptual categories and new modes of description are necessary to capture' the social feelings and material lives that are part of the experience of the contemporary world. And new categories and modes of description means pursuing a different kind of cultural study:

> This project's inquiry into depression, then, is also about new ways of doing cultural studies that move past the work of critique or the exposure of social constructions. Although I explore the history of depression as a cultural discourse and the pervasive widespread contemporary representation of it as a medical disease that can be treated pharmacologically, this book is not primarily a critique of that discourse. Instead, I seek to use depression as an entry point into a different kind of cultural studies, one with an interest in how we might track affective life in all its complexity and in what kinds of representations might do justice to its social meanings.
>
> (Cvetkovich 2012: 13–14)

Old forms of analysis that would critically work on depression as a 'distant object' that can be shown to be a social and cultural construction (a condition with a history, a discourse, an expertise that accompanies it) are avoided, and instead a close-up description of the culture of depressions as a singular yet collective experience is pursued. Such work, just like some of the artworks discussed at the end of the previous chapter, are not just works to admire, or discuss, or argue about; they are models that refashion the apparatus of the study of culture, and should be adopted and adapted. Such work should be absorbed into a changing canon of experiential maps that we can use to pursue our own cultural analyses.

Another model of the study of culture is provided in an essay by Jennifer Carlson and Kathleen Stewart. In their essay they explore how 'mood' exists in minuscule gestures and actions, repeated again and again over years. These are not individual moods but lived responses to the social conditions of cultural life. They constitute an atmosphere, an ambience that permeates habits and routines, and flavours anything from a trip to the supermarket to an annual family holiday. These atmospheres are the way we live our history. For Carlson and Stewart the task is to make these moods legible. The essay pursues two mood worlds: the first is the post-war US 'Good Life' as it is lived out across the 1950s through into subsequent periods; the second is the mood worlds of semi-rural German life as it is reworked as an 'economic miracle' that wants to employ technological solutions to daily life.

Like Perec in *Things* (but without his satirical bent) the authors take singular experiences to guide them through the legibilities of mood. Such work doesn't require the analysis of a 'cross section of the public' or a representative sample, it requires a close-up description of singular lives. In one section named 'Abstellraum' (which translates as storeroom or pantry) the authors (or one of them) is involved with clearing out the house of 'Oma', an elderly neighbour who has died. The *abstellraum* is a cellar where Oma stored her groceries and the jams and pickles that she made. When the neighbours came to clear it out it was stuffed full:

> Each object was part of an invisible line of movement between the kitchen and the cellar, paths Oma had traced as she cored and canned the fruits, unbagging the grocery store cans and stacking them on the shelves, the newspapers that she cut up after reading them with Opa [her husband] upstairs. The labor of everyday life thrummed through the cans and jars and the shelves themselves, in the preservative that kept the potatoes free of eyes.
>
> (Carlson and Stewart 2014: 129)

This is not a general cellar, it is a singular cellar lived out in its particularity, but because of this it echoes with a particular cultural history which reverberates within a much larger history: 'her cellar tells a story of what it means to be increasingly flush, if not wealthy—flush with material things unheard of in previous decades, and flush with the expectation of material things. Material things were a promise but also a threat. The possibility of more to gain also indicated more to lose' (129–30). As a cultural practice keeping a stocked pantry was clearly not something limited to Oma, and yet it is only by trying to describe the actuality of Oma's cellar that we can get a sense of how the seemingly banal practice of keeping the pantry stocked might make legible something of what it was like to be of a certain age and to live through the postwar period of German history: 'The *Abstellraum* was a growing-in to history, a way of dwelling in a period of so-called economic promise and a bulwark against the threat of crisis' (130). That growing-in to history is culture from the inside. It is culture as a process of living feelings, living relationships. It is, I would argue, the level of culture as it is actually lived.

Carlson and Stewart are anthropologists working with an understanding of culture as social experience filtered through cultural forms. It is descriptive work that deals in particularities and singularities but it isn't work that stays at the level of 'the individual'. What Carlson and Stewart find is a world of social energies lived by people whose lives are intimately collective even when they experience something like 'competitive individualism'. Describing the affective world of North Americans living out the postwar 'good life' they write:

> The mood work of the good life was atmospheric and ambient but also intensely personal and not easily shed or replaced. It was what put people into circulation in their worlds. What inscribed individual bodies, bodies of desire, and bodies of social-material-technological design as the material-semiosis of life itself. It culled attention to forms of living and magnetised subjects to the work of sensing out what was, or what could be, emergent in objects, scenes of interiority, characters and landscapes. It suspended them in the thrall of a real, a perpetual motion machine. With an energetics that could surge or deflate, inspire or depress, it settled on bodies as the weight of the world. It was the company and substance of a life, the impetus for a common life, and also, therefore, a restricted legibility of the subject and the world. And it abandoned people.
>
> (Carlson and Stewart 2014: 122)

This is a dense passage, but what is being described is culture as 'intensely personal' but also historical, collective, and social. It is attendant on the writer of culture (cultural describers and analysts) to evoke this world of culture, to describe cultural feelings and tensions. It is here where the more descriptive forms of cultural analysis offer us a view of culture as a world lived through disappointments, hopes and habits. Such a sense of culture follows on logically from E. B. Tylor's notions that culture is 'beliefs, etc.' but it comes to quite different conclusions about the best way to register it, the best way to investigate it.

If Carlson and Stewart suggest that culture is lived through immaterial feelings that are constantly fashioned within material practices, the anthropologist C. Nadia Seremetakis reminds us that our immediate sensorial worlds are both emphatically material as well as being the product of history and discourse. The world we inhabit is cultural and it is a world of touch, smell, sound, taste and sight. Culture is not just meaning as a collection of ideas; it is also energies, sensorial matter, technologies, the experience of time, and so on. The world 'hits' us through noises, through the odours that surround us. The world is something that we can crash into, that can trip us up. Is this world also cultural? Here I think we have a key question with which to test the limits of the cultural. In the next chapter I will be looking at sickness, dying and death. At what point does 'culture' adequately name this world of experience, and at what point do we admit we are confronted by something that is outside the grasp of culture, something that short circuits the forms that culture makes readily available?

In an essay called 'The Memory of the Senses', Seremetakis begins with a memory of eating a peach:

> I grew up with the peach. It had a thin skin touched with fuzz, and soft matte off-white color alternating with rosy hues. *Rodhákino* was its name (*ródho* means rose). It was well rounded and smooth like a small clay vase, fitting perfectly into your palm. Its interior was firm yet moist, offering a soft resistance to the teeth. A bit sweet and a bit sour, it exuded a distinct fragrance.
>
> (Seremetakis 1996: 1)

This peach had a nickname too: 'the breast of Aphrodite'. For Seremetakis this peach had a particularity to it that marked it out as different from other Greek varieties of peaches (which also had particular names) and marked it as different from American peaches which were all just called peaches.

The story that Seremetakis tells is how the 'breast of Aphrodite' became a memory that was inscribed in her experience of home and abroad. Living abroad, studying in America the peach was a constant absence made explicit by the indifferent taste of peaches in the United States. Visiting home, the breast of Aphrodite brings with it a sensual reality of home, of Greece. The longer she lived in the US the more the tasting of the breast of Aphrodite was caught up in the memory of its flavours. Memory is not something that belongs to the past; it is entangled in our perception of the present through cultural experience. As time goes on this particular peach becomes harder and harder to find until it disappears. The breast of Aphrodite peach is caught up in the history of food standardisation, and European import of non-seasonal foods. And it is a victim of this history. As such the particularity of the breast of Aphrodite becomes a memory of a memory: Seremetakis remembers looking forward to tasting this particular peach as a flavour of time and of home. The flavour has 'gone', what is remembered is the memory of remembering its taste:

> There is no such thing as one moment of perception and then another of memory, representation or objectification. Mnemonic processes are intertwined with sensory order in such a manner as to render each perception a re-perception. Re-perception is the creation of meaning through the interplay, witnessing, and cross-metaphorization of co-implicated sensory spheres. Memory cannot be confined to a purely mentalist or subjective sphere. It is a culturally mediated material practice that is activated by embodied acts and semantically dense objects.
>
> (Seremetakis 1996: 9)

Memory and the senses are entangled within culture, and culture is the mediation of material experience within sensual realms that include a 'semantically dense object', in this case the peach and all the cultural connotations that accompany it. The peach is both insistently and obdurately material (a peach is a peach is a peach) while it is also caught up in cultural associations (one of which is the association of its nickname) and historical processes, which includes the historical changes produced in the name of food standardisation, changes in Greece's national identity and so on.

What Seremetakis offers with her example of her experience of eating a peach is a form of cultural description that moves through sensual particularity into reflexive thought that allows her to capture historical change operating at the level of everyday life. Culture, in this case, is up-close, living and intimate while it also connects experience to much larger cultural forms that can only be seen as cultural as they are caught within experience and *not* reduced to historical facts (Greece joined the European Community in 1981).

## CULTURAL AESTHETICS AND CULTURAL ANALYSIS

If culture, for Raymond Williams and for cultural studies more generally, is both the 'complex whole' of an anthropological approach and a myriad of cultural productions (songs, novels, menus and so on) then is there an approach that can and should be privileged when we attend to culture? Is the 'patterns' of culture approach enough to capture the flavour of a disappearing peach? One powerful strand of cultural anthropology has taken culture to be made up of signs that require deciphering. This is a form of cultural analysis which suggests that culture is primarily made up of semiotic material (signs that signify within cultural contexts) which requires interpretation. Semiotics, as an act of deciphering, often relies on the sense that culture trades in meaning and that its major signs are symbolic. Thus within culture an item of clothing is a symbol of something that is more than itself or other than itself. To some extent this is true and culture is filled with elements that can only be understood if you are familiar with cultural codes (for instance our ability to read road signals in another country). But as we have also seen to 'read' culture as a system of symbols can be hugely problematic especially when it is the cultural interpreter who is sitting outside of the culture under interpretation and declaring that such and such a piece of clothing is an 'ostentatious' symbol of religion.

Much of our life is spent not in the world of verbalised meanings and ideas but in a world of habits and routines, of sensual worlds of sounds and flavours, of movement and rhythms. These are not 'meaningless' though they are resistant to any immediate translation into a symbolic vocabulary or into a set of verbal meanings. Eating and dancing, for instance, once the very basis of anthropological attention (as culture-at-a-distance), is hard to translate into meaningful activity in quite the way that a semiotics of culture imagines. What do we make of the smells and flavours of our eating? Surely this is culture, but it isn't part of verbal culture and it requires an act of imaginative description to make it something more than a list of ingredients or a series of moments within the daily patterns of a household.

In this last section of this chapter I want to suggest that what is required is a description and analysis of culture as an aesthetic form. By that I don't mean that it should be judged in terms of its beauty, but in terms of its sensual affects. Practising aesthetic description will be a way of moving beyond a translation of culture into symbols, a way of attending to the materiality of culture as a phenomenon. The examples of Carlson, Cvetkovich, Seremetakis and Stewart are instances of aesthetic approaches to feelings, moods, senses and matter. To finish I want to consider music as something that the study of culture has difficulty explaining and describing.

In Achille Mbembe's account of 'Congolese Worlds of Sound' he proposes to undertake aesthetic description of Congolese popular music: 'by "aesthetic description" I mean an attempt to describe the totality of sensations, pleasures and energies provoked by a particular work, or set in motion in the subject listening or dancing to it' (2006: 63). The sensations, energies and pleasures provoked by the music constitute sensorial work, but it is only by linking one set of stimuli to a broader world of sensation that you get a sense of the social aesthetics of the music: 'its aesthetic signification is revealed through that which links that work to a world of sensations' (62).

In his essay Mbembe moves from detailed aesthetic analysis of particular songs and dances, to a history of popular music in the Congo and to the tragic and brutal history of the Congolese people facing generations of brutality and exploitation. Mbembe's major description works to connect a sonic register lived at a social level to the sonic register of the music. After explaining how the sensorial environment of Kinshasa is best rendered as noisy – both in relation to sounds (babies crying, car horns hooting and so on) and in relation to a sensual cacophony (of food smells, car exhausts, sewage) – Mbembe explains that:

> Congolese musical works dip abundantly into this culture of noise. As it happens, any sound in the Congo can be used if not as a musical sound, at least to create music. Often, musical sounds are based on imitations of natural or onomatopoeic sounds. Congolese artists use noise to modify sound understood as pure form. This does not make their music less instrumentally rich, as evidenced by the virtuosity of its guitars and other forms of instrumental improvisations. What noise adds to rhythm are those spasmodic eruptions that often break the stream of slow melodies.
>
> (Mbembe 2006: 76)

Mbembe links the everyday clatter of Kinshasa (car horns, transistor radios, crying) to the 'atalaku' – the worlds of screams – that Congolese music deploys:

> Mixed with words, soaring bursts from the guitar, the screams of the *atalaku*, the rhythm of the percussion and the shape of the melody, it is transformed into an image of the very doors of hell – ear-punching frenzy, groping disorder and energy; or instead it becomes an effusion of tears provoked by the haunting memory of mourning, by jubilation and the unchained outpouring of emotion, reflecting as much the hollow tolling of reality as the pending fulfilment of still-awaited promises – an interweaving of myriad figures where the beautiful and the ugly are intertwined in the image of life itself.
>
> (76)

It should be noted that Mbembe is using a set of rhetorical forms to describe this music, but he doesn't work through symbolism. The sound might be *like* the 'very doors of hell' but this music does not symbolise 'hell' – indeed it is much too joyous and mournful to be captured in a single analogy.

The aesthetic description of Congolese music works in close attention to the sensations conveyed by the music, the singing and the dancing and this connects this musical form to a living situation made up of daily noises and rhythms, everyday violence and brutality on a national level as well as to the history of this musical form and the history of the Congo. In the end when Mbembe describes the music in terms of tragedy we have already witnessed this at the level of syncopation, screams and guitars: 'behind the sounds, there is the expression of an existence in which exuberance and the gift of suffering go hand in hand with fierce and powerful desires. Because this society, so accustomed to atrocity, is playing with death, its music is both born out of tragedy and is nurtured by it' (92–93). Such an interpretation is the outcome of material sensorial description that has located its object not in a distant set of symbols but in the everyday landscape of popular music, social and political reality, and ordinary sense-worlds of street life.

Mbembe's attention to the sensual particularity of a sonic soundscape, alongside attention to the physical aspect of performance and dance, is not something that we just find in more experimental forms of ethnography, it is something that you also get in music journalism, particularly as it was practised in the 1970s, 1980s and 1990s by a 'school' of rock journalism that drew on new forms of journalism and swapped dispassionate, distanced views of the world, for passionate, empathetic, insider views of worlds of sounds. Indeed it might be that some of our best experiential maps of modern culture are not to be found amongst the carefully tendered groves of university writing, but in the more hit-and-miss world of long-form journalism. Such writing tends to be less burdened by internalised paranoia and footnotes (which sometimes amount to the same thing), more often caught up in the lively excitement of being in the midst of a cultural scene (whether musical or with a much wider understanding of the cultural).

Greil Marcus's accounts of live music stand as a good example of what can be achieved in describing music. Here he is describing the music of the punk group, the Slits:

> Nothing could keep up with it. Shouting and shrieking, out of guitar flailings the group finds a beat, makes a rhythm, begins to shape it; the rhythm gets away and they chase it down, overtake it, and keep

going. Squeaks, squeals, snarls, and whines – unmediated female noises never before heard as pop music – course through the air as the Slits march hand in hand through a storm they themselves have created. It's a performance of joy and revenge, an armed playground chant.

(Marcus 1997: 39)

This sense of music as a process, not as something finished and done with but as an on-going unfolding, is emphasised in his writing. The way he captures and imagines a rhythmic movement catching up with itself, and overtaking itself, describes the tumbling effect such music can have. Less metronomic and more scattered and evolving. It is accurate and rhetorical, but also it has the lightness of prose produced under deadlines, of having to file copy for the weekly press.

In his descriptions of the post-punk band, the Gang of Four, from the UK he is attentive to the funky rhythms that they fracture with stuttering guitar breaks ('the tunes are constructed out of jarring off-beats, crooked [ ... ] guitar' [Marcus 1994: 51]), but focuses on their live performance:

Gill [the guitarist] is still wary and alert, searching for the sniper. The instruments vanish behind him and he goes blank – and keeps playing, as if he can't afford to think. King [the singer], bent over his melodica, a reggae plastic horn, puts his whole body into the few skimpy notes the toy can produce (imagine Carlos Santana [a rock guitarist famous for long languorous guitar solos] going through his the-pain-of-the-universe-is-in-my-guitar routine, with a ukulele). Gill, staring over his shoulder, crashes into King. King spins to the opposite side of the stage, sights past Allen's moving screen [Allen is the bass player], and takes his mike back on the run. What it looked like was straightforward enough: the Odessa Steps montage in Eisenstein's *Potemkin*.

(Marcus 1994: 117)

Aesthetic description, which is what I think this is, isn't confined to a dry description of the world as it *appears*. It is an engaged world of culture from the inside, an empathetic attempt to describe how that world feels, to grasp for analogies and associations that might make it more vivid. It is a creative and inventive act. In explicitly evoking two reference points, one that the Gang of Four are seen in opposition to, namely the guitar playing of Carlos Santana, and the other which they are seen to resonate with, namely Sergei Eisenstein's landmark film of engaged aesthetics, *Battleship Potemkin* (1925), Marcus connects music and performance to a larger world of sensation.

I think that the world of cultural studies is generally under-attentive to aesthetic description, perhaps it is too associated with a world of leisured interest rather than urgent enquiry. But cultural studies to my mind at least needs to learn aesthetic description and learn to spend time at the level of describing the cultural phenomena it is attentive to. Otherwise the world of ordinary sensual culture – the world of food, of bodies, of the senses – will end up as simply carriers of interpretations that have already been decreed in advance by the sort of 'culture-at-a-distance' accounts that are offered by the large-scale theory of Foucault, Bourdieu and others – who, it must be said, spent their time trying to describe a world that they were uncovering, before they mapped out their interpretative schemas.

This work shouldn't necessarily see aesthetic description as an end point for grasping the cultural, but as a way into an enquiry that wants a dialectical understanding of the totality as something that registers at the level of the sensual detail. This will be an approach to culture that will need to use phenomenology as much as semiotics to try and evoke a world of sensual actuality. It will need to test its abilities in attending to experience, to food, to water, in trying to describe what it is like to sneeze or to ride a bike.

# 6

## DEATH

Death is cultural. What could be more obvious? Funerary practices differ between cultures. The rituals of dying and of death for people who follow Hinduism are distinctly different than for people who follow Islam. One insists on cremation, the other on burial. In some cultures there is no particular hurry to bury or cremate the body, in others it is crucial that the funeral is as soon after death as possible. The treatment of illness and dying vary according to medical practices and the beliefs ensconced within medical institutions. In the early 1990s there was a TV show about the trials and tribulations of the community of a fictional small town in Alaska. The show centred on the character of a sophisticated and highly ambitious New York doctor who has to work in the town for a certain period before he can return home. Needless to say he finds most of the residents eccentric, unsophisticated and prone to superstition. The residents find Joel (the doctor) interesting, but also eccentric with his over-reliance on scientific explanation. At one point a First Nation/Native American visits Joel to ask if he can observe him at work. Joel is fine with this until he discovers that the man is observing him to learn about 'alternative medicine'. For Joel western medicine is just medicine, scientifically based knowledge: it is everything else that is 'alternative'.

Death is cultural. It is accompanied by stories. Even in Joel's world of scientific rationality there must be stories. The Native American healer has stories, he has a cosmology. Joel, not so much. Or this is what he thinks. As he hands out painkillers and antidepressants they come with a minuscule narrative form: take two a day, if the symptoms persist or if you develop side-effects, seek medical advice. But the real narratives are elsewhere: in metaphors, in manners of speech, in ideas about sickness and health. In Susan Sontag's classic essay *Illness as Metaphor* she highlights the military language that surrounds cancer:

> The controlling metaphors in descriptions of cancer are, in fact, drawn [ ... ] from the language of warfare: every physician and every attentive patient is familiar with, if perhaps inured to, this military terminology. Thus, cancer cells do not simply multiply; they are 'invasive.' ('Malignant tumors invade even when they grow very slowly,' as one text book puts it.) Cancer cells 'colonize' from the original tumor to far sites in the body, first setting up tiny outposts ('micrometastases') whose presence is assumed, though cannot be detected. [ ... ] Treatment also has a military flavor. Radiotherapy uses the metaphors of aerial warfare; patients are 'bombarded' with toxic rays. And chemotherapy is chemical warfare, using poisons.
>
> (Sontag 1983: 68–69)

To die from cancer is to 'lose the battle'. The dead are those who have 'courageously fought a battle that they couldn't win'. Another soldier down, more troops lost. What could be more cultural than having to live and die a set of metaphors, a social cliché?

Death, of course, is not cultural. It is biology. It is massive traumas. It is flesh and it is deterioration. It is hearts that stop pumping blood to the brain. It is organ failure. It is the end. It turns life into matter that is going to decompose one way or another. And death renders life something other than cultural, something *creaturely*. The art critic Tom Lubbock, diagnosed with a malignant brain tumour, quotes the poet John Keats: 'I go among the Fields and catch a glimpse of a Stoat or a fieldmouse peeping out of the withered grass – the creature hath a purpose and its eyes are bright with it. I go amongst the buildings of a city and I see a Man hurrying along – to what? The creature hath a purpose and his eyes are bright with it' (Keats cited in Lubbock 2012: 18). In life we are as stoats and mice, but we don't see it. We share a vital connection with animals. What we don't share is culture.

Death is not cultural, it is only *perceived* through cultural eyes. But what then is the extent of this perception, this 'only perceived'? Does it too invade everything, colonising our experiences? If there is clearly a *beyond* culture, or a *before* culture – and death must surely answer this in the affirmative – then how do we access this? The world of medicine is not outside culture yet it points to a material existence that clearly isn't exhausted by culture. The world of the economy is not simply outside culture, but it has effects that would trump culture at every turn (as whole countries know when a vaccine is unaffordable, and as you or I would know if we were turned down for treatment that was too expensive or if some health insurance expired). If culture is *always* an aspect of our contact with reality, then to study culture is to be concerned with *how* we engage with this reality, how we make contact. But we, like scientists, economists, taxi drivers, rabbis, morticians, hairdressers and steeplejacks, are also interested in reality. It is where we live. What we can't expect is some pure discourse untrammelled by culture (that would make no sense). But neither should we want to embrace a way of thinking and working that reduces everything to culture. What we are looking for, I think, is a form of enquiry that is culturally sensitive but is not afraid to go in search of the real.

In this chapter I'm going to take some of the lessons from the previous chapters to write about death as a reality, even if it is a reality that is perceived through culture. Culture isn't some superficial varnish, of course, that coats the reality of experience; it is more constitutional than that. And reality isn't some sort of malleable phenomenon that can simply be shaped by culture. Culture mediates reality, and mediations break down, go awry and become overloaded. What follows is an experiment with experience as a way of acknowledging the real in culture, the 'beyond culture' of experience. The first part of the chapter includes some sections from a diary that I kept while my father was dying. To lose a parent when you are in your 50s is not an uncommon experience, indeed the death of our parents is one thing that the vast majority of people will have in common at some point – it is part of the 'usual' life course (our own death, of course, is something that we will *all* have in common one day). But the death of a parent is always singular, always exceeds the provision of cultural conventions. In the second part I want to draw on some other accounts of death and dying and see where it might be best to locate the cultural within these death scenes and to explore what it might be that a cultural study of death could engage with and what it might accomplish.

## FROM MY DIARY

During the last weeks and months of my father's fatal illness I kept a very rough diary of what was happening. In part it was a way of keeping on top of what various consultants and doctors had to say and the different advice that we were being given. But it was also a way of marking a significant period in my life (I don't normally keep a diary). And to be honest it was also something to do that wasn't simply waiting around for the next appointment, or the next meal, or the next visiting 'hour'. It was something to do after doing all the possible errands that there were to do. I have only selected a few scenes from this diary and not included much of the medical stuff. At the time when I was writing this, it was mainly notes, and half-finished sentences. I've tidied it up a good deal for inclusion here and added material to provide information about the larger context. I've given short headings and used italics to signal a different sort of writing voice.

### TESTS ...

*We have been driven over a hundred miles by taxi and put up for the night in a hotel (and this is all free on the National Health Service). My dad is in London with an appointment at the National Amyloidosis Centre. I'm his helper, wheeling his wheelchair through the surprisingly narrow corridors of the hospital. He has already been diagnosed with amyloidosis; we're here to see how extensive it is and what the future holds. Amyloidosis is his second diagnosis. The first was myeloma: a cancer of the bone marrow. We can't be sure that amyloidosis is a result of the myeloma or if the myeloma was a misdiagnosis. Both involve the bone marrow but it seems that amyloidosis is what is doing the most damage to him. Amyloidosis is the production of proteins folded in such a way that they no longer dissolve in the bloodstream. These are the amyloids and they form deposits in organs and tissue which are wrecked in the process. Most commonly affected organs are the heart and the kidneys. It is a killer and at the moment there is no known cure.*

*The National Amyloidosis Centre (NAC) is like a four star hotel sitting in the middle of a giant two star guest house. It is buried somewhere within the rambling wings of the Royal Free in Hampstead, London. It is a world away from the regional oncology wards where my dad had previously been receiving treatment. Here there are artworks on the freshly painted walls, you could help yourself to coffee and tea, and everything is scheduled to the minute and runs on time. There is waiting involved but this is because there is a battery of tests to go through, some of which involved an injection of a radio-isotope which needs time to take effect. Amyloidosis, it turns out, is a rare illness and the effects of the amyloids is a fairly new discovery. At the NAC they are involved in a massive research project that is linking the production of amyloids to Alzheimer's as well as to various forms of amyloidosis. The potential for drug discovery is huge. GlaxoSmithKline are waiting in the wings. Hence the plush carpet, the soothing artwork, the brand new scanners.*

*The first tests involve an echocardiogram and an ECG (an electrocardiogram). We're in a fairly dark room and I'm helping my dad take his jumper and shirt off. I haven't seen him unclothed for years. Not since I was a child. It is a shock. He is a large man, six foot four inches (193 cm) tall (or he was in his prime). His torso seems to be devoid of flesh. His arms are stick-thin. Everything looks as if it could break. When the heart tests are over he is given the radio-isotope injection and we are told that it will be an hour or so before the full-body scans for protein deposits can take place. We head off for something to eat.*

*Outside of the NAC we return to the labyrinthine world of an over-subscribed, slightly down-at-heal NHS. The contrast is striking. It is like a hundred other hospitals around the country made up of hundreds of tired-looking staff, gigantic canteens, and the 'walking wounded' assisted by their friends and relatives, gingerly navigating obstacles like fire doors. And on the walls endless instructions about not visiting if you have a stomach bug (this is good advice: I caught the norovirus in one of the gigantic regional hospitals when visiting my dad, and was violently sick on the train home).*

*After the various scans we have a consultation with one of the doctors who specialise in amyloidosis. She is a small British Asian doctor who has a superb manner: no condescension, or false over-familiarity (the chummy over-familiarity, which is meant to imply bonhomie but is often just bossy and patronising, doesn't sit at all well with my dad). She is very matter-of-fact, calm and seems very kind. She examines my dad. While he has no flesh on his upper body, his legs are the opposite. For a year they have been swollen, and now they are huge, and suppurating. His socks are permanently wet, and he can barely get shoes to fit. After she has examined him she asks me to dress my dad, to put his socks back on. I feel sorry for her as she goes to wash her hands. I feel sorry for my dad for the thousands of minor humiliations that he must be suffering.*

*She asks us some questions. She asks my dad how he is feeling. He's been through it all before. She explains what amyloidosis is. She asks if my dad has any questions. He does. It's the one he's been asking ever since he was diagnosed with myeloma: how long have I got? There is no way of asking this that doesn't bring to mind countless movies: OK doc give it me straight, how long have I got? And her response is surprisingly precise: two to three months without treatment. (In this she was surprisingly accurate, it was almost exactly two months later when he died. It turned out that the treatment didn't delay things at all.) My dad asks her how long he would have with treatment. Here she is hesitant. Of course she can't say, can't give assurances. Who knows? But we get the message, we get the picture. Treatment might delay things but there is an inevitability here. He will die fairly soon.*

*In the car returning us to my parents' home we talk about the consultation and about what the future holds. We talk about Angela – my mother – and about what she might be feeling. He thinks that she must be worried about money and about what she would do on her own. He talks about how easy it will be to sell the house and that she could then buy a flat somewhere in town or nearby. We talked about setting up accounts so that it is easy for her to access money. She will get just over half his pension. She will be alright financially.*

*The car is being driven in a fashion that makes it hard to con-centrate on what my dad is saying. The car is speeding up and slowing down constantly even though there doesn't seem to be any other cars on the road at this point. The car radio is playing and I hear the obituary of a sculptor who I am writing about: his son is on the radio telling us that his father had harboured a lifetime of guilt for the suicide of his father, who had killed himself during the Second World War not long after his wife (the sculptor's mother) had died. The reason for the guilt was due to the fact that the sculptor (though he wasn't one at the time) was a wartime pilot undergoing training and wasn't allowed time-off to attend his mother's funeral.*

*TIME SLOWS ...*

*Time crawls. I think it may have stopped altogether. I've never before felt so insistently the weight of time. Everything hangs heavily. The central heating is on too high. I whisper to myself those fateful words: 'I'm bored.' And immediately feel guilty. Boredom isn't the requisite feeling to have while administering to a dying parent and helping out at home. Boredom probably isn't the right word at all. It is something worse. We are waiting for him to die. No one says it of course. We are waiting for him to get better, or for him to have some remission. This is what we tell ourselves. No one had told me that time freezes when you administer to a dying parent.*

*I have fallen through a hole in time. There must be a little rent in the fabric of time and I've dropped through it. I'm now in a world where time moves with a sort of glacial plodding, interspersed with little bounds in time (sometimes forward, sometimes back). Sudden jolts of time can hurtle forward: so a small task, such as helping my father take a bath, can basically suck up the entire morning; activities that used to rush past pretty smoothly are now crawling by and perhaps actually reversing time. Meal times have become like that. And of course time has reversed for me. I'm thrown back to being a 'son' again, living at home, negotiating all the areas of conversation (such as politics) that have always caused massive rows.*

*I assumed that the TV would be my friend in all this. If I share little with my mum and dad in terms of the way we see the world, the one thing that used to be a fairly safe bet was telly: as long as it wasn't anything too controversial (the News, for instance) then TV was fine. I hadn't quite cottoned on to their new diet of TV: the TV zone that is called 'early evening dramas', but seems to last all evening. This is an endless diet of repeated dramas from the world of middle-England. You are now in a broadcast world that is pointed firmly at some point in the past; there should be warning messages telling young people to turn off, warning those who might be worried that they are getting on a bit to turn around now before they get sucked into the whirlpool of* Poirot, Heartbeat *and* Bergerac. *These are dramas with layers of nostalgia: for a time when they were made; to the time before that – the period that they represent. This is the world of tea shops and vicars, a world where murder isn't bloody – just genteel. The energy is ebbing out of the world in hour-long episodes.*

*We watch* Coronation Street *which is a soap opera that has been going since 1961 (the year of my birth, the year that the Berlin Wall was erected). My mother and father have watched it since it began. As I sit and watch there are people I recognise from my childhood – Ken Barlow, the resident intellectual, one of the few to attend university from this imaginary street. It didn't take him far, of course …*

## STOPPING TREATMENT …

*We have gone to visit the heart consultant. We rehearse it many times. To get our story straight. If there are no signs of improvement and if the prognosis isn't optimistic at all, then my dad is going to stop treatment. I'm happy to back him up with this. He doesn't want to keep going. The chemo is making him feel terrible. They had to stop the last chemo sessions because his heart isn't strong enough for it. (While amyloidosis isn't a form of cancer, you treat it with the same cocktail of treatments as you would for a cancer.) It isn't far to the hospital where the consultant works and we get picked up in an ambulance. It is an ambulance that already has about four other old men in it being taken to various places. The ambulance crew bundle my dad into the ambulance. He cries out that he is going to fall. They say jovially, that it's alright 'young man' we've got you. I can feel him seethe. Actually he seems to be past that. Humiliation isn't there for him anymore. Just the memory of feeling condescended to. I can't bear to hear him cry out. I can't intervene either: they are doing their job and doing it professionally (he doesn't fall).*

*We are with the consultant in his office. One of the things I notice is that he has his computer screen in a portrait format rather than in a landscape format (like a mobile phone rather than like a TV). Perhaps this is the way forward. Perhaps all those videos made on vertically held iPhones are in the correct ratio for this future. Perhaps it is the best way to look at medical files. He tries to get my dad's details on the computer, but in the end he has to go to the main office and print them off there. The consultant takes us through the results of my father's recent heart tests: the amyloids have damaged his heart and he can't have chemo; the prognosis isn't looking good and there is no telling when or if he will get to the point where they will be able to continue chemo. My dad says the words – 'in that case then I don't want to carry on with any treatment'. The consultant considers this – he is looking for the sentence structure that he has used a number of times before – one that says that you have made the right decision without saying you have made the right decision. This way he can stay true to his Hippocratic Oath but also give my dad the reassurance he needs about his decision. I can't remember the words precisely, they were something like 'I don't think that in the circumstances you are making a wrong decision'. Double negatives can work wonders. We are grateful to him. My dad feels like he has taken back some control of his life.*

*We wait an absolute age for the ambulance to arrive and take us back to my mum and dad's house. It is several hours. The journey home in the ambulance is even worse. He really thinks he will fall, he is beside himself, he is crying out. I should have booked a taxi instead. It would have been much quicker, much easier. I should be able to drive, then none of this would be happening. It is the worst journey.*

## THE GUTS HAVE GONE OUT OF ME ...

*I have been back home (back to my home) for a few days and then a phone call. We had spent ages persuading the hospital that my dad should be allowed to come home. He was fed up with being in hospital and hated the food there. So we got him home. But now he has lost his nerve and wants to go back to hospital again. Carers come in a couple of times a day (one of them is a wonderful woman originally from Rumania who is also training to become a psychiatric nurse) to help him wash and dress. But he is worried that he will fall when no one is there apart from my diminutive 88-year-old mother. So I hurry back there to help.*

*He has been crying, my mother tells me. I don't know what to do with this information. Nor does she. When I talk to him he tells me that 'the guts have gone out of me'. He has no life force. For years he would always do the Sudoku puzzles in the paper. He did them in hospital. They kept his mind sharp, he thought. He was probably right. But now they don't interest him. The stuffing, the guts have gone. He wants to go. He asks doctors if they could do something to hasten the going. But they laugh it off and say it's not in their gift.*

*The hospital has a bed for him and can readmit him. It will take a few hours. He decides that a plan he had to make this year's batch of marmalade should go ahead and that he can direct the proceedings from his sick bed downstairs. I'm dispatched to buy the requisite number of Seville oranges and mountains of sugar. My mother is there too: she is sterilizing the jam jars with boiling water. The oranges and sugar are bubbling on the stove like a cauldron of angry lava. It is frighteningly hot.*

*The ambulance crew comes in the middle of it all. They have to move furniture to get their gurney in. I help but have to keep one eye on the marmalade. The carers are there too. There are crowds milling around, it seems. And the oranges are bubbling. He is in the ambulance and I ride with him to the hospital to get him settled. By the time I'm back from the hospital my mother has bottled all the marmalade. This batch will last her for well over a year. She gives some of it away. Eating for one makes it last a lot longer.*

*I wonder why, at the point that life was leaving him, he insisted on this marmalade production. I guess it was to have some way of contributing to continuity, of providing for a future that wouldn't include him.*

## IN THE KINGDOM OF THE SICK

> Illness is the night-side of life, a more onerous citizenship. Everyone who is born holds dual citizenship, in the kingdom of the well and in the kingdom of the sick. Although we all prefer to use only the good passport, sooner or later each of us is obliged, at least for a spell, to identify ourselves as citizens of the other place.
>
> (Sontag 1983: 7)

Culture haunts death, but death pulls the rug from under culture. Death confronts us with an unmanageable real. It presents us with suppurating flesh and asks us to deal with it, to manage it within our cultural codes. If culture is our habit world and our conventional world, then death threatens to make nothing of our habits. It is the ultimate de-habituating act. Of course for doctors, nurses, palliative care givers, and hospice workers, such an act as dying is absorbed into habit, into routine, into conventions of speech ('my condolences', 'perhaps you need to take a minute – take all the time you need'). Just as birth punctures the conventions of culture for new parents, if only for a while, it clearly wouldn't have that effect if your daily work is as an obstetrician or midwife.

What is and isn't cultural in the diary entries above? Clearly there is much that is to do with society at large and which has cultural forms of expression. The fact that care was being offered under the National Health Service (NHS) rather than as part of a private health insurance is important. It links this specific example with a national history that goes back to the Second World War and to the post-war constitution of the Welfare State and the National Health Service. Huge hospitals such as the Royal Free, as well as regional hospitals that also treated my dad, are the result of decisions that were (and are) economic, medical, architectural and logistical. Such decisions result in cultural experiences that will be familiar to many people who have used large NHS hospitals: the endless corridors; the feeling of getting lost; and the sense of being within a huge medical machine. With it also comes much more personal feelings, which would be affected by media representations of the NHS, the experience of the care you have received, your sense of the priorities of the department that is treating you or your loved one, and so on. Culture operates across car parks and news headlines, corridors and consultation rooms. The ideal would be a sense that the best medical decisions are being made, and made without a concern for profit (though with some concern for cost). (Though the possibility of profit is what makes the National Amyloidosis Centre so much plusher than the rest of the hospital.) These are historical, political, cultural experiences: how much longer will the NHS survive as a not-for-profit institution of care for all 'from the cradle to the grave'?

Large metropolitan hospitals are perhaps the most cosmopolitan places you can find in the UK (alongside airports). Without migrants and a multicultural population it is hard to imagine the NHS functioning, and certainly my dad's care was consistently multicultural at every level (South Asian British for doctors; East European for nursing). My father died at a moment when there was a rising tide of anti-immigration politics in British politics which was concentrated in the rise of the political party UKIP (the United Kingdom Independence Party), a right-wing party made up of disaffected Conservatives who want an end to the European Union and to the current immigration policies. On the morning after two UKIP members were elected to parliament, the Labour politician Dennis Skinner spoke in parliament about Labour's role in resurrecting a badly damaged NHS that had been returned to the pinnacle of achievements: 'I've got a United Nations heart bypass to prove it, and it was done by a Syrian cardiologist, a Malaysian surgeon, a Dutch doctor, a Nigerian registrar, and these two people here [the two new UKIP MPs] talk about sending them back from whence they came' (*Independent*, 21 November 2014). These are political–cultural aspects that impact on the hospital experiences (and would, I hope, make anyone who has experienced the care of the NHS side with Skinner against UKIP's xenophobic policies).

Alongside (and running underneath) these elements that relate to a national culture are all sorts of cultural framings that connect to more personal (though still deeply social) culture: family, class, generation. My diary is the diary of a son witnessing the demise of his father, a father that had been brought up in the 1930s and 1940s within strict middle-class manners and customs, where parents were figures of love, authority and guidance rather than friendship. We got on fine, he was an incredibly supportive parent, but feelings were not something that were ever going to be explored by either of us at any length. Events such as family bereavement and illness take you into the heart of the affective entanglements of family life: the feelings of love, but also of frustration, of sadness, of guilt. The diary alludes to a degree of awkwardness in talking about death, of talking about a time after death. It registers the paternalism of a man who is a father and a husband, who wants a familial world to carry on operating in his care after he has gone.

But culture is the operation of all these factors, and more, when the world is running smoothly. Culture is there to stop things breaking down. But bodies do break down. Culture is there to prop us up when things go wrong: it offers us frameworks for coping with catastrophe, for explaining to ourselves what is happening and how we should be feeling. The outside of culture is those feelings that can't be contained within these frameworks, the bodily dispensations that rail against the protocols that are already in place. I cried a lot. I often felt sick.

## TEACHING DEATH

When the art critic Tom Lubbock was diagnosed with an incurable brain tumour he reflected on the lack of teaching that there was available to prepare for death. In western modernity death isn't a subject for reflection; it is an enemy to overcome. For the anthropologist Paul Stoller, finding out that he had cancer returned him to his training as a sorcerer with the Songhay people in West Africa:

> Most Americans don't like to think too much about death. Many of us can't even accept inevitable changes to our aging bodies, a sign that life is finite, let alone the specter of death. In the world of sorcery, however, illness is ever present in life. In that world, illness is a gateway to learning more about life. As for death, it is your continuous companion.
>
> (Stoller 2004: 39)

Stoller's knowledge and practice of Songhay sorcery gave him a different cultural framework for conceptualising and living with what was happening to his body. For Lubbock the choices were more limited:

1. To face the inevitable when it should come, trusting medicine, hoping for the best, recognising the goodness of my life as long as it might prove to be.
2. To do everything possible to prolong my life, to pursue every path, to concentrate all my thoughts on this object.
3. To fill my time with real pleasure and new and intense experience – the round-the-world-trip, the last hurrah, or whatever; I'm going to enjoy it.

(Lubbock 2012: 97)

He chooses the first option. Many choose the second or third. These are culturally prescribed choices – passive acceptance, aggressive refusal, hedonistic abandonment. They are also personal choices.

Lubbock's deterioration through his illness offers us a glimpse of the edges of culture. His tumour was located in the particular part of the brain that processes language. As his condition deteriorates he finds it harder and harder to grasp certain words, to construct sentences, to spell words he knows well. His fluency leaves him. But what is most damaged is not the complex technical languages of art criticism (his professional language), or the languages of self-reflexive thought, but the everyday language that gets used automatically:

The problem is mainly in idiomatic, clichéd, everyday talk. And the speech that requires more attentive or inventive language comes out right. One is more aware of what one says. The speech that goes wrong is the speech that should actually deliver itself quite correctly, automatically, unthinkingly. It was already there to be said. And the fact that it goes wrong makes it clear that its normally reliable mechanism has failed. Unless I really slow down and pay attention, it will go wrong quite often.

(Lubbock 2012: 32)

This might offer us one of the most useful definitions of culture: culture is what is 'already there to be said'. Culture is our habits of mind, our habits of language, the things we routinely say (the things that are there waiting to be said), what we routinely think (that which is already there to be thought). And this is why when we talk about the dominant metaphors that describe the processes of illness (particularly in relation to cancer) we are talking not about a way of dressing experience (as one way of describing an actuality that is prior to the metaphor used to describe it), but as something fundamentally entangled with how we experience the world. The metaphors of 'battle' of 'fighting' cancer are there before the diagnosis.

In Lubbock's case the common way of speaking, the culturally shaped phrases and sayings were lost. In this sense his words became unmoored from culture. His wife, the artist Marion Coutts, described his language choices as normally paced, but jumbled, or careful and considered but unusually slow:

> We discuss strategies. One is to verbally go for broke. Tom could learn to accept a percentage of nonsense in the interests of volubility in a sort of trade, not waiting to get things right but crashing in, usurping the speech habits of a lifetime. He has noticed that he can sometimes get more done by taking a jump at language, not going so much for style. It is the automatic bits that are the problem. It might have diminishing returns but it is a way. This will be hard for him. It is a Blurters' manifesto. To be truly comprehensible, everything he says has to be thought out first. He must think very hard before he speaks. We, who do not think before we speak, speak, and the thought is there, full-spake, articulate. It sits like jelly on a plate before us.
>
> (Coutts 2014: 131)

To be self-reflexive, to have to think about everything isn't to have access to a pure outside of culture, but it does put culture at a distance, allow you to inhabit it as a stranger (which is a massive inconvenience). It is similar to the slow purposeful way that we operate when we visit an unfamiliar country and we don't know the language. We aren't inside culture in the way we are when we are operating in our native tongue. Culture in this sense is an amazing set of accomplishments, but like habit it also makes us blind to alternative ways of operating. And finding alternatives might be something that western cultures need to do for figuring a world where more and more people will live longer and longer, and where dying will need to be something that requires more than automatic responses.

In his book *Being Mortal: Illness, Medicine and What Matters in the End*, the medical writer and surgeon Atul Gawande is concerned with the way that metropolitan culture treats illness and dying as something that should simply be overcome. It is not a sustainable position of course. Death is the one thing we can all be sure of: as Samuel Beckett put it, 'Birth was the death of him' (Beckett 2006: 263). Birth is a guarantee of our death. For Gawande the problem is that western societies have placed so much faith in curing illness that we may have traded-in the possibility of having the death we want and the death our loved ones might want, for a death that can only be conceived of as a *medical* experience. The medicalisation of death, Gawande notes, is a fairly recent option: 'this experiment of making mortality a medical experience is just decades old. It is young. And the evidence is it is failing' (Gawande 2014: 9). Gawande has spent his career working in hospitals and he has witnessed the way that 'the waning days of our lives are given over to treatments that addle our brains and sap our bodies for a sliver's chance of benefit. They are spent in institutions – nursing homes and intensive care units – where regimented, anonymous routines cut us off from all the things that matter to us in life' (Gawande 2014: 9).

This way of dying, whereby older people who need a modicum of help in looking after themselves are given over to forms of incarceration which keep them safe but where their freedom is severely truncated by the routines of staff and the protocols of an institution, is a cultural form that is dominant within many countries today. And if the illness is more catastrophic (rather than the general decrepitude of the faculties), many of us can look forward to an end where we are hooked-up to machines, and administered through tubes. Gawande tells us that other cultural forms exist, for instance his grandfather lived to be nearly 110 living on his farm in rural India. Up until the final year of his life he would ride a horse around the entirety of his farm before going to bed. Though he was relatively fit he still needed looking after. He was cared for by his children and grandchildren in a way where he could maintain his independence and still have a good quality of life.

Gawande's book is filled with different ways of looking at illness and death and suggests that within the 'complex whole' of culture there are often a range of positions that can be adopted. He tells of how he spent time working with a geriatrician at a Center for Older Adult Health, where a 85-year-old woman (Jean Gavrilles) presented a number of health issues: arthritis, lower back pain, glaucoma, slight incontinence, and a lung nodule that could be a metastasis of a colon cancer that she had previously had surgery for. For Gawande the most urgent tasks were to deal with the possible cancer and the back pain: for the geriatrician what was important was to maintain a quality of life and independence for Gavrilles. Because she had a number of conditions, she was on a complex drug regimen that was making her dehydrated (which was partly causing the incontinence) and making her dizzy. After talking to her for some time and examining her feet the geriatrician could see that she was losing weight and that her feet were painfully sore. Her greatest danger was from falling and breaking a hip and losing her independence. What the geriatrics team did was to get her seen regularly by a podiatrist and to simplify her medications, making sure that diuretic medicines were swapped for non-diuretic ones: 'they saw that arthritis was controlled. They made sure toenails were trimmed and meals were square. They looked for worrisome signs of isolation and had a social worker check that the patient's home was safe' (Gawande 2014: 45). In other words the geriatricians treated the whole person not the individual medical conditions (though of course she would still need to see an oncologist about her lung node).

In another part of the book he tells us about a doctor, Bill Thomas, who took up a position as the medical director at a nursing home, where many of the residents were severely disabled and where most had some form of dementia. When he arrived what he saw depressed him hugely, he saw a 'home' of boredom, loneliness and helplessness. In trying to find a remedy for this lifeless institution Thomas' intuition was to introduce some life into it. This he did by introducing animals, plants, and children into the everyday life of the institution:

> That fall [1991] they moved in a greyhound named Target, a lapdog named Ginger, the four cats, and the birds [one hundred parakeets]. They threw out all their artificial plants and put live plants in every room. Staff members brought their kids to hang out after school; friends and family put in a garden at the back of the home and a playground for the kids.
>
> (Gawande 2014: 120)

The experiment required getting special permission from the local authority who saw animals as a safety issue and a health hazard. The results were staggering. Patients who hadn't spoken for months started to talk, those who barely moved would offer to take a dog for a walk. After noticing such dramatic changes in the nursing home a group of health researchers compared this newly enlivened nursing home to a comparable one nearby. The results showed that the number of deaths had fallen by about 15 per cent since the plants, animals and children were introduced, and that the use of drugs (particularly drugs for anxiety and agitation) was just '38 percent of the comparison facility' (Gawande 2014: 123).

Residents who had disengaged with the world around them became re-engaged, animated by the lives of others. All the parakeets were given names and looked after by both the residents and the carers. In some essential way Thomas' experiment changed the culture of the institution. In another way he worked to de-culture the place:

> This task was not small. Every place has a deep-seated culture as to how things are done. 'Culture is the sum total of shared habits and expectations,' Thomas told me. As he saw it, habits and expectations had made institutional routines and safety greater priorities than living a good life and had prevented the nursing home from successfully bringing in even one dog to live with the residents. He wanted to bring in enough animals, plants, and children to make them a regular part of every nursing home resident's life. Inevitably the settled routines of the staff would be disrupted, but then wasn't that part of the aim?

'Culture has tremendous inertia,' he said. 'That's why it's culture. It works because it lasts. Culture strangles innovation in the crib.'

(Gawande 2014: 119–20)

This experiment, then, isn't just a practical parable about how we can make institutions more liveable for older people who need constant care, it shows us something about the nature of culture and the limits of culture.

By introducing animals and other lively beings into a context that was primarily geared to low levels of liveliness, which were materialised through drug routines, quietness, and safety procedures, the experiment broke with culture. This doesn't mean that another culture wasn't introduced (indeed it was reliant on a cultural norm: that particular groups of people want to care for dogs, cats and parakeets). It means that culture includes within itself a tendency to ossify through habitual repetitions. Simply to alter habits is to break with culture, even if culture is itself in the process of being re-orchestrated.

It is here where we find a critical dynamic for the study of culture. Our entry point in the investigation of culture is often here at the moment of interruption, at the moment when a hundred parakeets turn up at a nursing home, the moment when illness jeopardises your routine accommodations with the world around you and requires you to make them anew, the moment when your father's body deteriorates in front of your eyes. It is at such moments that we see culture because we also see it fall away. To study culture (as a formal student of cultural studies, or as an informal student of life) is to de-culture it. And this means attending to the singular moment, which, when seen in detail, is itself an act of de-culturing.

In the final months of my father's life he asked me a few times to cut his hair for him. He didn't have much hair, and what he had was white and wispy. I'm no hairdresser but all he required was a trim to stop his hair from sticking out over his ears. I used an electric trimmer and a comb and the excess hair seemed to roll off in little snowy balls of fluff. Both times that I cut his hair were full of tenderness. I don't think I had ever paid so much attention to his body, his materiality, his being. There was something there in those wispy strands of hair, something monumental that I could hold on to. It was both being and non-being.

Culture tells us how to deal with death, what rituals to perform, what ceremonies to arrange. It tells us that it is alright to be sad, to cry, to be mournful. It gives us a choice of ways of disposing of a body. It edges around us, showing us how to behave, how to think, but our actuality exceeds it. Culture seeks to reabsorb our experiences within its sometimes lively, sometimes sclerotic forms, and to some extent it will always do this. But the singularity of life will always provide moments when culture falls away. What are we to make of such moments? Will we feel at a loss when this happens or newly alive? Is death always the negation of life, or something else? To confront death as part of life is what the dominant culture of medicalisation makes exceedingly hard: as a medical problem death is always failure. But that is not necessarily the best way to live and certainly no way to die.

The affect theorist, textile artist and founding voice of queer theory, the late Eve Kosofsky Sedgwick, lived within the grasp of death for about thirteen years when she learnt that an earlier treated breast cancer had metastasised in her spine. She expected to live with this diagnosis for a maximum of three years but it turned out to be a much more 'indolent' cancer than had been predicted. For Sedgwick her textile practice became tangled up with her proximity to death, a way of living with death's intimacy. Living with her diagnosis meant confronting what the reality of death might mean:

> ... the imperative to try and wrap my mind around the reality of death, what it might mean both in itself and for how I'd live whatever long or short time remained of my life, became suddenly very material and pressing, in a way I don't think it tends to be for healthy people in their forties. That sense of urgent and even exciting intimacy with nonbeing, intimacy with the kind of questions it asks of life, built itself more and more into the center of my understanding, and particularly my practice of art.
>
> (Sedgwick 2011: 70)

The word 'exciting' is witness to the falling away of culture. For Sedgwick, death's proximity meant attuning yourself to what non-being could possibly be, and in recognising the logical contradiction in such a consideration (non-being can't be).

To grasp the complex whole of life (including non-life) is culture's remit. It always falls short. And in falling short we get to see culture, we get to test its limits. And what is it that is on the other side of culture that exceeds it? We could call it life, or singularity, we could even call it the lively energy of death.

# 7

## TWO CHEERS FOR CULTURE?

The English novelist E.M. Forster titled his 1951 collection of essays *Two Cheers for Democracy*. The title points to his assessment of democracy which deserves 'two cheers', which 'are quite enough: there is no occasion to give three' (Forster 1951: 78). For Forster democracy 'is less hateful than other contemporary forms of government, and to that extent it deserves our support' (77). I am not interested here in Forster's assessment of democracy but I do want to borrow his formulation. Culture, it seems, is something we can't do without but it might be 'quite enough' to give it only two cheers. What I want is a more modest sense of what we can study in the name of culture, and where we need to admit to the limitations of a culturalist perspective. But I also want a more ambitious (ambitious but not bombastic) form of cultural study, one that works in the name of addressing reality rather than just addressing the ways that we point at reality.

I hope it is clear by now that while the term 'a cultural construction' may do some initial work in reminding us that we live in a world that we have inherited, a world that has shapes and patterns through which we experience life, it is a paltry goal if our only aim is simply to reveal these patterns and shapes *as* constructions. Such a goal is highlighted within popular culture as something that is lacking in empathy or life experience. In the popular TV series *The Big Bang Theory*, which revolves around the lives of various 'science geeks', the phrase is used to show the absurdity of the ultra-rationalism of some of the group. In episode five from season four, Sheldon Cooper is worried that his relationship with Amy Farrah Fowler is moving on to the next level (she has asked him to meet her mother). Just when he decides to terminate their relationship Amy assures him that this is just a ruse to satisfy her mother's concerns:

Sheldon: And you haven't fallen hopelessly in love with me?
Amy: Don't be absurd. I find the notion of romantic love to be an unnecessary cultural construct that adds no value to human relationships.
Sheldon: Amy Farrah Fowler, that's the most pragmatic thing anyone has ever said to me.

The joke is partly that it would be very hard 'to fall hopelessly in love' with Sheldon, and partly that such a rationalist and pragmatic approach to amorous relationships would be understood by many as simply a disavowal of the complexity and irrationality of human sexual relationships. But the humour is also based on the fact that we understand Sheldon's lack of empathy and we empathise with it, we understand that Amy's words could ironically sound highly seductive to Sheldon who clearly has Asperger's Syndrome and therefore can't read human emotion or anything that is not entirely literal (sarcasm, for instance).

To claim something as a 'cultural construction' is little use in explaining the power that culture has, the way it both constitutes our experiential skin and gets under it. It does not help us describe the world as it is inhabited by creaturely beings living complex entanglements with other human beings and other creatures, with the environment, and with assemblages of objects. To claim something as a 'cultural construction' might offer a way of de-naturalising the world, but it is a gesture that quickly loses its capacity to provoke critical enquiry. It too easily slips into another way of keeping the world at a distance.

I hope it is also clear by now that reserving the term 'culture' for items that a certain group of cognoscenti find beautiful and spiritually uplifting is unhelpful and often a form of class privilege. Thus I would want to reject the use of 'culture' when it is deployed by Forster to denote beauty and interest:

> Culture is a forbidding word. I have to use it, knowing of none better, to describe the various beautiful and interesting objects which men have made in the past, and handed down to us, and which some of us are hoping to hand on. Many people despise them. They argue with force that cultural stuff takes up a great deal of room and time, and had better be scrapped, and they argue with less force that we live in a new world which has been wiped clean by science and cannot profit by tradition.
>
> (Forster 1951: 108)

But rejecting this use of culture is not to reject beauty or interest, nor is it to reject selection. I think we constantly need to make claims for beauty, for interest, and for all sorts of moody, affective states, for ugliness, for awkwardness, and so on. I also think that we, as analysts of culture, need to be more openly discursive about how and why we select the kinds of texts we do. Is it inevitable that bibliographies will contain a list of the current favourites of social and cultural theory? What other ways of modelling our approaches to culture are there?

As a way of concluding this book I want to raise two cheers for culture and the study of culture by offering four topics that, I think, require a self-reflexive vigilance at the moment, but which are also themes that are an invitation to conduct a more open and inventive form for studying culture. The first of these is the question of 'cultural reductionism'; the inclination that everything in the world can be explained by starting out with the phrase 'it's cultural'. I want to think about the way that we could guard against cultural reductionism. Second, I want to suggest that the most powerful aspect of cultural investigation is that it allows us access to what I would call 'collective intimacy', that is our collective life but seen from the inside, as a felt, experiential realm. Now I think that accounts of collective life and intimate life are both relatively common (you could point to social history for examples of collective life and diaries, autobiography and biography for intimate life), what is more difficult is to do both at once. The third topic I want to broach, and one related to the previous topic, is to discuss the possibilities of finding a productive distance for studying culture. Is there a correct, critical distance for producing productive accounts of culture, or are we destined to constantly zig-zag between the close-up and the long-shot? Lastly, but perhaps most importantly, I want to suggest that studies of culture, because of the huge remit that this could cover, need to be clear about why they matter. I'm not suggesting that all studies need to have a political urgency to them, but that they should be clear about why a cultural form or a cultural instance is being singled out for scrutiny and why they are being scrutinised in a particular manner.

## GUARDING AGAINST CULTURAL REDUCTIONISM

One of the major problems with the avariciousness of culture as a form of explanation is that it is based on a tautology (a tautology that I mentioned at the start of this book): if culture is the 'web of meanings' that humans create, and if the only meaningful things in the world are meanings, then *all* we have is culture as a realm of explanation. In this way culture short-circuits enquiry: it is a way of knowing the explanation in advance, because the question has posed the terms of its own answer. We ask 'are there cultural reasons why the world is experienced in this particular way?' and the answer always comes back: 'it's cultural'. Today there are lots of arenas where such an answer is politically and epistemologically deeply problematic. Climate change is the most obvious case.

The sociologist of science, Bruno Latour, has spent his career showing how 'incontrovertible facts' within science worlds were the result of all sorts of decisions and conventions that determined how some things counted as 'facts' while others did not. If the protocols were changed, so were the facts. In more recent years he has found a version of his argument being used by interested parties keen to deny the links between human-produced pollutants and climate change. For 'climate change deniers', as it was for generations of critical cultural sociologists, the world is a matter of

interpretation rather than a matter of fact. And it is in the interests of those whose fortunes are tied to fossil fuel consumption
that doubt is thrown in the face of scientific consensus. For
Latour there is now a problematic connection between those who
use the terms of cultural and social constructionism to challenge the
powerful explanations of the world that dress historical contingencies
in the garb of nature, and those who challenge the people who
challenge powerful explanations of the world:

> Entire Ph.D. programs are still running to make sure that good
> American kids are learning the hard way that facts are made up, that
> there is no such thing as natural, unmediated, unbiased access to
> truth, that we are always prisoners of language, that we always speak
> from a particular standpoint, and so on, while dangerous extremists
> are using the very same argument of social construction [or cultural
> construction] to destroy hard-won evidence that could save our lives.
>
> (Latour 2004: 153)

The answer is clearly not to return to an uncritical acceptance of
science or those who speak in its name. But nor is it adequate for
those who seek to understand the world to reach for the cultural
as the 'trump' explanation of how the world is.

A more modest assessment of what cultural forms of enquiry
can offer progressive investigations should be accompanied by a
more open and generous interest in other forms of knowledge and
other forms of understanding. Opening up cultural enquiry to
psychology, neuroscience, genetics, geology, economics and so on,
is one way of avoiding cultural reductionism, and consequently of
providing much more substantial accounts of cultural processes.
As the political philosopher William E. Connolly argued, some
cultural theorists shy away from biological understandings of
human life because they are worried about forms of genetic
determinism and a consequent lack of interest in human cultural
creativity. Yet by not engaging with the sciences of the body and
the brain they might be actually lessening the scope of how we can
understand cultural creativity: 'cultural reductionism – that is, the
minimization of how biology and culture are always mixed together
in human life – threatens to generate the results its practitioners

fear. It depreciates the layered character of the body/brain/culture network and thus ignores some aspects of that network implicated in cultural creativity' (Connolly 2006: 67). Looking more broadly at psychology and neurosciences will not result in the marginalisation of culture and cultural explanations. What it will do is show how deeply entangled what we call 'culture' (behaviours, beliefs, habits, values, emotions and so on) is with networks of neurons, muscle groups and biological affordances.

The other aspect of cultural reductionism that needs vigilance is the tendency of culturalism to contract the world into smaller and smaller groupings of identity and to lose sight of the ambition of cultural enquiry to study life in terms of 'complex wholes'. As Catherine Gallagher argues, there is a tendency to reach for the term culture as a way of insisting on specificity:

> We tend to use the adjective *cultural* when we want to indicate that the phenomenon we are describing is both externally and internally generated (i.e., social and psychological, in old-fashioned terms), material and symbolic, class- and gender-specific, specific also as to ethnicity, race, religion, language group, region, profession, nationality, historical period, and so on. *Cultural* is a world-conjuring adjective; you cannot go wrong when you call something cultural, for it is the one term that, without specifying anything, carries the full weight of all possible forms of specificity.
>
> (Gallagher 1995: 309)

In one sense, then, culture is used to guard against sloppy generalisations or forms of universalism that do not stand up to scrutiny. So for instance a redress to a claim that 'people are naturally greedy' might quite rightly want to point out that while this might seem to be a truism for a group who have been taught that competition is an essential aspect of life, it is not true for other forms of social organisation. The desire for cultural specificity is a healthy way of insisting on a materialist approach to understanding human life.

But where do we locate specificity? If we locate specificity at the level of the group, then we also need to ask what we mean by a group. The way specificity has been used as a 'cultural form' has been to associate group with identity, and the more that specificity is insisted on the more identity is narrowed. The danger here is that contradiction, conflict within identity, and within the heterogeneous material associations that we inhabit, gets traded for something more abstract and in the end more solipsistic. One response to the abstractions of cultural specificity in terms of notions of pure identity is to insist that people, particularly those that suffer discrimination and social injustice, live across identities, and that we cannot hope to understand the complexity of this if we look at gender, race, class, age, etc., as isolated phenomena. Thus to account for an African American woman's experience it isn't enough to look at sexism and then to look at racism as impacting on her life, you would want to look at how such forces intersect. Intersectionality is the term that is often used to describe this way of offering more complex accounts of social and cultural life (Crenshaw 1991).

Guarding against cultural reductionism might mean swapping cultural specificity in terms of 'identity', for an approach that favours cultural singularity as a way of attending to material actuality as one case amongst others. Singularity, here, does not mean individualism, far from it. Instead it insists on attending to a particular instance or realm of cultural life without the safety net of imagining that this will immediately embody patterns of life already known and named. Singularity can include the conventional and those aspects where culture falls away. Singularity can include the insistent reality of deteriorating flesh and the medical culture that tries to frame it. There is always a world beyond culture, even if that 'beyond' can be reabsorbed within it or rendered as unspeakable:

> Men and women do not live by culture alone, not even in the more capacious sense of the term. There is always that within culture which baffles and balks it, twists it into violent or nonsensical speech, or deposits within it a residue of sheer meaninglessness. [ ... ] Whatever puts culture in place and perpetually threatens to undo it can only, so to speak, be reconstructed backwards once culture has already happened. In this sense, to be sure, it does not escape meaning; but neither is it reducible to the symbolic realm.
>
> (Eagleton 2000: 107)

To explore the world of culture as both a symbolic realm and as a refusal of symbolism is, I think, the most productive way of pursuing the study of culture. I will have more suggestions about how this approach to culture can be beneficial in the section below on distance. It is also relevant to the discussion of the next section.

## EMBRACING COLLECTIVE INTIMACIES

There are, I think, two aspects of the study of culture that together make it worthy of attention. It is what separates culture from society (not perfectly, but in emphasis) on the one hand, and what separates the cultural from the more purely artistic (again not perfectly) on the other. The word society posits a social body of people and institutions – it is a mass body, united and divided by forms of government, by hierarchies and status. Society is that enormous assemblage of institutional arrangements (school, work, family, military, and so on) that run the gamut from rigorously formal to improvised and informal. Much of what takes place at the level of society is cultural, but the cultural suggests an 'inside' of society: beliefs, feelings, differences, phobias, anxieties. There is a good deal of overlap here of course, and many people who practise cultural studies could just as easily be doing cultural sociology or cultural anthropology.

Similarly the artistic, certainly in the period designated as modernism, is often interested in what the world feels like from the inside: in those phobias, beliefs, anxieties, pleasures, trepidations, and so on, with which we greet the world and the world greets us. The work of art (particularly as a dramatic form) rarely strays from the desire to be as true as possible to this world, though this has often meant striving to find new, and to some ears decidedly odd, mechanisms for doing so (fragmented narratives, 'stream of consciousness' prose, and so on). Yet even if veracity to experience is a goal, dramatic art isn't governed by a responsibility towards representing society as a 'whole way of life' or as a complex whole (though some of it does precisely this). We, as readers, are the ones that make connections across the specific worlds being shown to us, we are the ones who decide if such a rendering of experience is true, or adequate, or lacking.

The study of culture navigates between these poles, trying hard to hang on to the energy of attempts to render experience as vividly lived, while also taking responsibility for connecting experiences to social forces. In this it tries to cling on to the world as it is lived at an intimate level (a level of proximity to the senses, to affects, to materiality) *and* a collective level. When we enter the world of experience (especially intense feeling) it might often feel that we are alone, that what we are experiencing is something like 'pure subjectivity'. Yet our experience of reading novels and watching films, of listening to people describe their feelings and how the world seems to them, is often an experience of recognition: yes this is how I feel too. If there was no recognition in the realm of cultural representations then I can't imagine that there would be such a thing.

One of the issues that we face, especially in cultures that have pursued capitalist development extensively over centuries, is that our culture is partly characterised by the word 'individualism'. Indeed one influential political theorist describes the origins of capitalism with the terms 'possessive individualism'. For C. B. Macpherson in *Political Theory of Possessive Individualism: Hobbes to Locke*, a form of individualism was promoted that coincided with property acquisition as a social goal: 'its possessive quality is found in its conception of the individual as essentially the proprietor of his [or her] own person or capacities, owing nothing to society for them' (3). Within a culture of possessive individualism ideas such as 'personality' or 'genius' obscure the shared social world we inhabit and the way that it acts on experience. In many ways individualism has been extended since the era that Macpherson is writing about: competition, fragmentation, and separation have been intensified.

But the experience of individualism is contradictory. We might be constantly pressed to be 'ourselves', to be 'unique', but the agencies who are pressing us in this way tend to want us all to buy their products to prove how unique we are. In this we are all in the same boat. We all share the culture of individualism as a collectivity, even though we are alienated from this collectivity through the ideology of individualism. In a digital world these contradictions find even more emphatic forms of highly selective communities on social networks who might share a huge amount of similar likes and dislikes, of cultural references, and values, and yet see this as enhancing their individuality rather than recognising how much of self-making is a collective effort.

By 'collective intimacies' then I mean the world of feelings, the senses (the tastes, sounds, and so on, and their connected feelings of pleasure, indifference and disgust), emotions, moods and fantasy. This is the world close-up; but it is a close-up world that we share. This proximate world is experienced most directly and we often feel that this is the world that is most individualised, yet it is also here that we can see the way culture and society have sensitised us and dulled us in particular ways. The world of the senses is neither the universal world of shared human capacities, nor the individuated world where each sensate subject is unique:

> Our own sensory experience provides an essential basis for exploring ways of sensing. However, it is inadequate to rely solely on personal experience for understanding how people everywhere perceive the world. While humans share the same basic sensory capacities, these are developed and understood in different ways. Some of this diversity is based on individual differences, such as the ear training a musician undergoes, but much of it is the consequence of general social conditioning.
>
> (Howes and Classen 2014: 8–9)

Here, we should note, that even the experience of 'individual differences' would be shared amongst those musicians who had received a similar ear training.

But 'collective intimacy' also conjures up a sense of the world of attachments: between people; in ways of presenting yourself; in forms of affection; in worlds of attraction. These are sensory and affective attunements and they are both public and counter-public (those forms that aren't so easily shared in public, or are counter to the hegemonic forms of condoned intimacy). This is a world that Lauren Berlant calls 'transpersonal identities and subjectivities', and charting them is a way of bringing to the surface forms of life that have particular importance for the study of culture (for instance the experience of debt, or the experience of demonised subjectivities):

> How can we think about the ways attachments make people public, producing transpersonal identities and subjectivities, when those attachments come from within spaces as varied as those of domestic intimacy, state policy, and mass-mediated experiences of intensely disruptive crises? And what have these formative encounters to do with the effects of other, less institutionalized events, which might take place on the street, on the phone, in fantasy, at work, but rarely register as anything but residue? Intimacy names the enigma of this range of attachments, and more; and it poses a question of scale that links the instability of individual lives to the trajectories of the collective.
>
> (Berlant 2000: 2–3)

Berlant's work on intimacy is a way of making vivid forms of collectivity that can appear invisible or vacant. These aren't shared cultural identities but shared affective roles that are forever conjured in the nightmares of the mass media in phrases such as 'benefit scrounger', 'lazy immigrant' and so on. The social isn't just there in large aggregates of people who share the same social background and the same political disposition. It is also there in the collective intimacies of the cultural, in the details of our attunements and attractions, our affections and distractions.

## FINDING PRODUCTIVE DISTANCE

The first thing to say here is that there is no *correct* distance for studying culture. There isn't a perfect focal length whereby culture as a tangled complex whole comes into critical focus, where we can see the most important lines of cultural energy emerge, and dense fields of cultural force become vivid. In an essay on methodology and cultural studies Anna McCarthy points to the ways that any distance, near, far or median, is liable for criticism because it fails to take into consideration alternative perspectives. She is imagining a non-specific cultural conference where:

> You can attend a panel of world system historians in the morning and chide them for the absence of 'voices' in their accounts, and then criticize a panel of ethnomethodologists and microhistorians for disregarding the big picture in the afternoon. In each instance, what you

are calling for is an impossible thing: a research stance that affords a total view, and which is able to move effortlessly between scales. You are asking, in other words, for a researcher who embodies the ideal liberal subject, capable of synthesizing all forms of knowledge, and a research program capable of absorbing all epistemological perspectives.

(McCarthy 2006: 26)

The perfect distance is an impossible stance, an impossible scale. Instead we are caught oscillating between the near and the distant.

Literary theory, for instance, has for many decades promoted the practice of 'close-reading', a way of attending to texts in close-up. Sometimes the unit for close-reading isn't even a whole novel but a passage within it that is given the most scrupulous and speculative probing. But at the same time those working within literary studies have always had a sense of the survey, of large historical sweeps that recognise the long histories in which something like the emergence of the novel is fairly precisely located as an event within literature. Today close-reading is challenged by what Franco Moretti calls 'distant-reading':

A new object of study: instead of concrete, individual works, a trio of artificial constructs – graphs, maps, and trees – in which the reality of the text undergoes a process of deliberate reduction and abstraction. 'Distant reading', I have once called this approach; where distance is however not an obstacle, but *a specific form of knowledge*: fewer elements, hence a sharper sense of their overall interconnection. Shape, relations, structures. Forms. Models.

(Moretti 2005: 1)

Moretti's approach to distant-reading is clearly fit for an age of computers, of 'big-data' and large research teams (and, of course, the grants that go with them). It is a scale of operations that is fashioned for the digital humanities and an age of globalisation.

Scale and distance present us with a choice that is partly determined by historical circumstances. What are we going to choose: the close-up view, which might allow more empathetic engagement, which might suggest a more complex entanglement between analysts and analysed, which might work more intricately to get a sense of specificity to an object and its relation to a context? Or should we work more distantly, use the estranging effects that otherness produces, and which allow us to see culture differently and might allow us to see culture as not just complex but as a *whole* way of life? Is there a middle ground here, a perspective which is neither too close, nor too far, which might include an ambivalence within its viewpoint?

McCarthy's essay on scale and method suggests that in the past those working within cultural studies purposefully produced research objects that complicated the separation of distance and proximity. For McCarthy the idea of the 'ordinary' became a research object that could be aimed at those scholars whose viewpoint was particularly 'lofty' and distant: 'New Left cultural critics, historians, and sociologists fashioned ordinariness into a deliberately small-scale conceptual object that was not only to be studied but also lobbed over the walls of the disciplines and institutions of higher learning' (34). In the 1950s and 1960s to look at ordinariness was to offer a counter-scale to those engaged in the study of elite forms (high-culture, political elites, or as mirror image 'deviants, recidivists, and perverts' for a more torrid sociological imagination). But the ordinary wasn't simply a form that *only* demanded an attention to detail through close-up inspection. The ordinary was 'the small scale of lived experience' and also the large scale of common experience: 'as a concept, *ordinariness* thus served a political purpose within academic research programs by disrupting conventional assumptions about scale and value, generality and importance' (34).

This tradition has been continued since the 1950s, and characterises an approach to the study of culture through attention to everyday life. This is culture lived in all its moment-to-moment particularity, but with a sense that it constitutes a grammar of practices (not just a series of isolated irreducible examples). This approach to culture often takes its lead from the French theorist Michel de Certeau whose *Practice of Everyday Life* sought to establish an approach to culture as a 'science of singularity': 'for what I really wish to work out is *a science of singularity*; that is to say, a science of the relationship that links everyday pursuits to particular circumstances. [ ... ] The characteristically subtle logic of these "ordinary" activities comes to light only in the details' (de Certeau 1984: ix). This might sound as if it is an approach that favours the close-up over the distant, but here we need to pay attention to the choice of words: 'science' and 'logic'. These terms suggest a much larger scale, a sense of distance whereby singular experiences and specific practices can be seen as forms and styles that share properties with other singular experiences and specific practices.

What such approaches offer is a way of studying culture that isn't forced to remain forever at the level of the micro-analytic, where experience or text is irreducibly a particular instance of itself, and where one example cannot connect to other examples within a much larger firmament. But this approach is also a way of avoiding the God-view which would see particular instances of experience as just another example of what it has already deemed as significant. A 'science of singularity' would not have to remain within de Certeau's interests of discovering a logic of practice, it could work with affective states, sensorial worlds, economic relationships (the world of chronic debt, long-term illness, forms of childcare, etc.) and work to draw connections across experiences with the intention of elucidating 'something' of the totality.

To move from the singular world of experience and performance (textual or otherwise), towards an idea of totality that can never be fully elucidated and which includes a myriad of singularities, offers an approach that can hold on to empathy and can remain responsive to the singular as lived experience. Such a way of understanding culture as a dialectic of an insufficient singularity and a speculated and unknowable totality, is, I think, the most productive way of approaching culture. In this dialectic culture is the mediational form that allows connections to be made between irreducible actuality (actuality that exceeds the terms of culture, to some degree at least) and the social totality that is culture in its ultimate unknowable state. Such a dialectic is most adequate for attending to the level in which we live, and it is the most generative in contributing to how we can think about culture in relation to a totality of relations and forces. And it allows us to engage with the world in a way that makes culture matter, not as politics, nor as sociology but as culture.

## ENGAGING WITH CULTURE THAT MATTERS

Culture matters more so than ever. Today people fight one another in civil and uncivil wars in the name of culture: because of long historical enmities; because of different interpretations of sacred texts; because of different ways of conducting their affairs. Culture is continually drifting into other forms that are also cultural: religion; politics; economics. These things matter. The study of culture allows lots of things to matter. They are not all measured by the same sense of urgency that would be appropriate to discussions about funding for health provision, for instance, or whether more money should be spent on foreign aid. Just as culture has different scales of visibility, it also has different rhythms and durations. Cultural analysts sometimes want to react to the immediate cultural crises that are always blooming around them, and sometimes they want to take a longer view. In this very last section I want to suggest three cultural themes that matter (to me, at least) and to suggest three counter-intuitive objects for exploring them. All three favour the longer view rather than the shorter view, but this is just my preference.

I will dispense with the first theme very quickly as it was the content of the final part of the last section. I think that what matters in exploring culture is the totality. I think that understanding the world should always be the ambition for the study of culture however wide of the mark we might fall in our attempts to register it. I do not want to pursue a form of cultural study that is happy offering just a slightly better interpretation of a film or a more adequate account of a cultural ritual. But I also do not want to be part of an enterprise that treats living cultural experiences and complex cultural utterances as mere reflections of a totality that exists fully formed and can absorb all within its wake. I want to gesture towards an unknowable totality by being attentive to the tone and manner of culture at the level of its living detail and actuality. So if it is the totality that matters then my response is to go and find it in the singularity of culture.

The second theme that matters is the present. But to attend to the world as it is in the present means necessarily working historically. You can have little inkling whether something is old or new, a recent trajectory or a retrofitted one, unless you can work with a sense of the history of the present. In a recent book that looks to rework the idea of formalist analysis as a way of connecting representations to social phenomena (because they both orchestrate the world into forms and patterns), Caroline Levine writes that:

> The most historically minded scholars choose to study gender norms in ancient Rome or eighteenth-century global commodity routes precisely because comparable arrangements of power operate now: because gender and commodity forms still organise us, carrying their pain and injustice with them; because distributions of authority and goods continue to restrict life and labor; and because we can reflect on the contingency of our own ordering principles when we know that they have at other times been organized otherwise.
>
> (Levine 2015: xii)

This succinctly describes the dual role that historical work plays in the study of culture in the name of the present: the past both connects and disconnects to the present, and in both its connecting and disconnecting it makes important critical resonances with the present. History demonstrates continuity and discontinuity and in doing so it shows how the present is not an inevitability. We don't always have to arrange things in the same way, there have been different ways of conducting ourselves, of valuing each other and exploiting each other.

But just as history can be made to resonate with the present, it also exists in the present. Current culture is filled with history, and not just in the name of heritage. What we call culture in terms of patterns of habits and beliefs is often another name for memory. Cultural memory is both what is remembered, but also what does not need to be remembered because it is absorbed within us as habit. Particular ways of doing things, ways of greeting each other, leisure activities (football, for instance) are forms that we have inherited from the past, that we have absorbed into daily life and which we pass on to future generations. Culture is both traditions and innovations, both memory and invention.

But the past exists in the present not just as our cultural unconscious, not just as models to follow and inhabit, it also exists as a threat. Particular historical periods exist in the present as a set of values and warnings: 'our finest hour', 'our darkest days'. The 1960s, for instance, exist in the present as a set of warnings about what can go wrong if we let idealism overcome common sense (this is what 'common sense' or ideology tells us is bad). The 1960s as an imagined past is there to warn against experimental education, permissive society (though that horse may well have run), and inhumane housing. That this is an ideological construction that works in the interests of those who want to maintain particular social forms means that the dominant understanding of history as it exists in the present is the understanding of the dominant class and dominant forms of thought. The 1970s are there to remind you what happens if workers have some control over their lives. If this is a warning its ideological identity should be even more vivid.

Culture, as a selective tradition, is a powerful force in deploying historical scenes (repackaged as heritage and horror) for the purpose of cultural hegemony. And just as we need to work culturally to include material that runs counter to the selective tradition in the arts and in thought, so too do we need to provide counter historical narratives as a way of countering the hegemonic understandings of the past that are used to undergird the present. As Raymond Williams suggests the important thing here is to make sure the connections are emphasised:

> It is significant that much of the most accessible and influential work of the counter-hegemony is historical: the recovery of discarded areas or the redress of selective and reductive interpretations. But this in turn has little effect unless the lines to the present, in the actual process of the selective tradition, are clearly and actively traced. [ ... ] It is at the vital points of *connection*, where a version of the past is used to ratify the present and to indicate directions for the future, that a selective tradition is at once powerful and vulnerable. Powerful because it is so skilled in making active selective connections, dismissing those it does not want as 'out of date', or 'nostalgic', attacking those it cannot incorporate as 'unprecedented' or 'alien'. Vulnerable because the real record is effectively recoverable, and many of the alternative or opposing practical continuities are still available.
>
> (Williams 1977: 116)

So if the present matters, the way to make this mattering concrete is by working historically and by drawing the past into the present and the present into the past as a way of clarifying current phenomena, and by showing that the present is not the inevitable outcome of human development.

The final theme is the human being: what it means to be human. If humanness matters, and I think this is why we study culture, then to look for the human might mean turning away from the 'person' and looking at the edges of human life. To look at humans face-on is often to be caught in our own reflection, as if the human is already known. But we should know to be careful here, to recognise that this is the most likely place for cultural hegemony to operate. We are, after all, fashioned from inherited thoughts and images that tell us that the individual is what matters, and that the human self is fashioned into a thing called 'personality'. If we want to see humanness as a product of culture, and as an interruption within it, then we might do better to try and steal up on the human, to take it by surprise, to look at it askance. It might be better to see the human from the perspective of the animal and the thing.

How do animals look at us? What do they see while they thread their way around their enclosures at the zoo waiting for food? What do our pets tell us about ourselves when they curl up on our laps, or bark at the postman? What does our system of manufacturing meat tell us about our relationship to different animals? And what do the giraffes make of a Land Rover filled with camera-wielding tourists visiting their safari park? We can't know, of course, what animals think (or if 'thinking' would be an appropriate way of imagining an animal's response to the human world) but we can work to see how animals in their various roles (as pets, as wild animals, as food) have constituted human–animal worlds.

For John Berger, in his classic essay 'Why Look at Animals?', the progressive marginalisation of the physical animal in human life is accompanied by the transformation of animals into images (the animal-shaped toy, the zoo, the safari, the nature documentary) and a fantasised companion (the pet):

> In the past, families of all classes kept domestic animals because they served a useful purpose – guard dogs, hunting dogs, mice-killing cats,

> and so on. The practice of keeping animals regardless of their use-fulness, the keeping, exactly, of *pets* [ ... ] is a modern innovation, and, on the social scale on which it exists today, is unique. It is part of the universal but personal withdrawal into the private small family unit, decorated or furnished with mementoes from the outside world, which is such a distinguishing feature of consumer society.
>
> (Berger 1977: 12)

Looking at animals, and the long history of human–animal relations, tells us something about the changes that have taken place within human culture, and it tells us something about the cultural worlds that we have created that allow us to look at animals in particular ways (and which only allow them to look back in particular ways too).

But if Berger tells a story about human–animal relations as a dominant narrative of loss, Donna Haraway offers us a more complex account of what she calls 'companion species' in which the term 'pet' is not precise enough to describe the various ways we have of living with animals. For Haraway the history of animal–human life (and in particular dog–human life) is heterogeneous in the extreme:

> For the nineteenth-century Comanche of the Great Plains, horses were of great practical value. But horses were treated in a utilitarian way, while dogs, kept as pets, merited fond stories and warriors mourned their deaths. Some dogs were and are vermin; some were and are buried like people. Contemporary Navajo herding dogs relate to their landscape, their sheep, their people, coyotes, and dog or human strangers in historically specific ways. In cities, villages, and rural areas all over the world, many dogs live parallel lives among people, more or less tolerated, sometimes used and sometimes abused. No one term can do justice to this history.
>
> (Haraway 2003: 13–14)

Nor is there a particular quality of attachment that can describe human–animal relations. To describe a relationship as 'love' when it involves misrecognising a dog as something like a furry human baby offers an infantilised form of love. Similarly, to refuse the description 'love' when describing the trust and respect that a farmer might have for a working dog is also to see love as primarily an infantilised form. Looking at animals, then, could tell us a good deal about what humans mean by love in relation to cultural differences.

Just as we can't really look at the human being with animal eyes, so too we can't quite see the human world from the perspective of a rock or a table. Yet seeing how rocks and tables have been figured within human culture is a productively critical way of finding out how human life is differentiated *from* a world of things, while also being implicated in the transformation of the world of things (transforming trees into tables, turning rocks into sculpture). It is as transformers of the material world that human culture is fashioned, and the way 'things' circulate is a crucial way of characterising cultures. In the social form known as capitalism, for instance, the crucial aspect of things is the form that they take as commodities. Commodities are, for Marx, magical objects where exploitation and labour time have been disguised, and rendered into an intangible quality. Thus the commodity 'is nothing but the definite social relation between men themselves which assumes here, for them, the fantastic form of a relation between things' (Marx 1988 [1867]: 165).

But the commodity form only describes one aspect of contemporary capitalist culture in its relation to things. For writers such as Bill Brown the object in its thing-form (i.e. as a form shorn of its commodity status) offers the possibility of telling other stories about modern life. He suggests examining literature in terms of:

> How it renders a life of things that is tangential to our narratives of modern production, distribution, and consumption; how it can contribute to a materialist phenomenology that does not bracket history, but asks both *how*, in history (how, in one cultural formation), human subjects and material objects constitute one another, and *what* remains outside the regularities of that constitution that can disrupt the cultural memory of modernity and modernism.
>
> (Brown 2003: 402)

Again by looking at things, not in terms of how they are presented by those that promote them (advertisers, for instance) but by those who are drawn to their obduracy, we get to see human-kind from the sides. It is in the matter of culture – its concrete, material practices of constituting worlds of habits (habits of mind and physical habits) and when those worlds of habit break down – that we will find the culture that matters.

Culture, I hope I have shown, is a term built around conflict and confusion. In itself it is not an analytic term, or a particularly useful one. It is however a term that is alive in the world and needs constant critical scrutiny. Culture can become an analytic form only through making choices about the techniques for attending to it as an amorphous but ultimately limited field.

# BIBLIOGRAPHY

## BOOKS

Abu-Lughod, Lila (2002) 'Do Muslim Women Really Need Saving? Anthropological Reflections on Cultural Relativism and Its Others', *American Anthropologist*, Vol. 104, No. 3, pp. 783–90.

Armitage, John, Ryan Bishop and Douglas Kellner (2005) 'Introducing Cultural Politics', *Cultural Politics*, Vol. 1, No. 1, p. 1.

Arnold, Matthew (2006 [1869]) *Culture and Anarchy*, Oxford: Oxford University Press.

Bailey, Victor (1994) 'Review' (*The Rise of Popular Literacy in Victorian England: The Influence of Private Choice and Public Policy* by David F. Mitch), *History of Education Quarterly*, Vol. 34, No. 1, pp. 89–91.

Barber, Bruce, ed. (2008) *Condé and Beveridge: Class Works*, Halifax: Press of the Nova Scotia College of Art and Design.

Barrell, John (2014) 'At Tate Britain', *London Review of Books*, Vol. 36, No. 24, pp. 34–35.

Barthes, Roland (1973 [1957]) *Mythologies*, translated by Annette Lavers, London: Granada.

Becker, Howard (2001) 'Georges Perec's Experiments in Social Description', *Ethnography*, Vol. 2, No. 1, pp. 63–76.

Beckett, Samuel (2006) *Collected Shorter Plays*, London: Faber and Faber.

Benedict, Ruth (1934) *Patterns of Culture*, Boston: Houghton Mifflin Company.

Benjamin, Walter (1931) 'A Small History of Photography', in *One Way Street and Other Writings*, London: Verso, 1985, pp. 240–57.

——(1934) 'The Author as Producer', in *Understanding Brecht*, London: Verso, 1983, pp. 85–103.

Berger, John (1977) 'Why Look at Animals?' in *About Looking*, London: Writers and Readers, 1980, pp. 1–26.

Berlant, Lauren, ed. (2000) *Intimacy*, Chicago: University of Chicago Press.

Brown, Bill (2003) 'The Secret Life of Things: Virginia Woolf and the Matter of Modernism', in *Aesthetic Subjects*, edited by Pamela R. Matthews and David McWhirter, Minneapolis: University of Minnesota Press, pp. 397–430.

Brown, Steven D. (2002) 'Michel Serres Science, Translation and the Logic of the Parasite',*Theory, Culture & Society*, Vol. 19, No. 3, pp. 1–27.

Bruner, Edward M. (1986) 'Experience and Its Expressions' in *The Anthropology of Experience*, edited by Victor Turner and Edward Bruner, Urbana: University of Illinois Press, pp. 3–30.

Carlson, Jennifer D and Kathleen C. Stewart (2014) 'The Legibilities of Mood Work', *New Formations*, Vol. 82, pp. 114–33.

Clark, T. J. (1985) *The Painting of Modern Life: Paris in the Art of Manet and his Followers*, London: Thames and Hudson.

Connolly, William E (2006) 'Experience and Experiment', *Daedalus*, Vol. 135, No. 3, pp. 67–75.

Coutts, Marion (2014) *The Iceberg: A Memoir*, London: Atlantic Books.

Crenshaw, Kimberlé Williams (1991) 'Mapping the Margins: Intersectionality, Identity Politics, and Violence against Women of Color', *Stanford Law Review*, Vol. 43, No. 6, pp. 1241–99.

Cvetkovich, Ann (2012) *Depression: A Public Feeling*, Durham: Duke University Press.

Darwin, John (2009) *The Empire Project: The Rise and Fall of the British World-System, 1830–1970*, Cambridge: Cambridge University Press.

de Certeau, Michel (1984) *The Practice of Everyday Life*, Berkeley: University of California Press.

Derrida, Jacques (1988) *Limited Inc*, Evanston: Northwestern University Press.

Douglas, Mary (1991 [1966]) *Purity and Danger: An analysis of the concepts of pollution and taboo*, London: Routledge.

Dwyer, Claire (2008) 'The Geographies of Veiling: Muslim Women in Britain', *Geography*, Vol. 93, No. 3, pp. 140–47.

Eagleton, Terry (2000) *The Idea of Culture*, Oxford: Blackwell.

Eliot, T. S. (1962 [1948]) *Notes Towards the Definition of Culture*, London: Faber and Faber.

Fabian, Johannes (1983) *Time and the Other: How Anthropology Makes Its Object*, New York: Columbia University Press.

Forster, E. M. (1965 [1951]) *Two Cheers for Democracy*, Harmondsworth: Penguin.

Frazer, James (2009 [1890]) *The Golden Bough: A Study in Magic and Religion*, Oxford: Oxford University Press.

Gallagher, Catherine (1995) 'Raymond Williams and Cultural Studies', in *Cultural Materialism: On Raymond Williams*, Minneapolis: University of Minnesota Press, pp. 307–19.

Gawande, Atul (2014) *Being Mortal: Illness, Medicine and What Matters in the End*, London: Profile.

Geertz, Clifford (1973) *The Interpretation of Cultures: Selected Essays*, London: Fontana Press.

Green, Nicholas (1990) *The Spectacle of Nature: Landscape and Bourgeois Culture in Nineteenth-Century France*, Manchester: Manchester University Press.

Greenblatt, Stephen (1995) 'Culture' in *Critical Terms for Literary Study*, edited by Frank Lentricchia and Thomas McLaughlin, second edition, Chicago: University of Chicago Press, pp. 225–32.

Greenhalgh, Paul (2011) *Fair World: A History of World's Fairs and Expositions from London to Shanghai 1851–2010*, Winterbourne: Papadakis.

Grusin, Richard (2004) *Culture, Technology, and the Creation of America's National Parks*, Cambridge: Cambridge University Press.

Haraway, Donna (2003) *The Companion Species Manifesto: Dogs, People and Significant Otherness*, Chicago: Prickly Paradigm Press.

Howes, David and Constance Classen (2014) *Ways of Sensing: Understanding the Senses in Society*, Abingdon: Routledge.

Jameson, Fredric (1993) 'On "Cultural Studies"', *Social Text*, Vol. 34, pp. 17–52.

Jardine, Nicholas, James Secord and Emma Spary, eds. (1996) *Cultures of Natural History*, Cambridge: Cambridge University Press.

Killian, Caitlin (2003) 'The Other Side of the Veil: North African Women in France Respond to the Headscarf Affair', *Gender and Society*, Vol. 17, No. 4, pp. 567–90.

Knausgaard, Karl Ove (2014) *A Death in the Family (My Struggle: 1)*, London: Vintage.

Kushner, Marilyn S. (2002) 'Exhibiting Art at the American National Exhibition in Moscow, 1959: Domestic Politics and Cultural Diplomacy', *Journal of Cold War Studies*, Vol. 4, No. 1, pp. 6–26.

Latour, Bruno (2004) 'Why Has Critique Run out of Steam?: From Matters of Fact to Matters of Concern', in *Things*, edited by Bill Brown, Chicago: University of Chicago Press, pp. 151–73.

Leavis, F. R. (1972 [1948]) *The Great Tradition*, London: Pelican.

Levine, Caroline (2015) *Forms: Whole, Rhythm, Hierarchy, Network*, Princeton: Princeton University Press.

London, Jack (2005 [1903]) *The Call of the Wild*, London: Kingfisher.

Lubbock, Tom (2012) *Until Further Notice, I Am Alive*, London: Granta.

Marcus, Greil (1994) *In the Fascist Bathroom: Writings on Punk 1977–1992*, London: Penguin.

——(1997) *Lipstick Traces: A Secret History of the Twentieth Century*, London: Picador.

Marx, Karl (1988 [1876]) *Capital: Volume 1*, London: Penguin.

Marx, Karl and Frederick Engels (1970 [1846]) *The German Ideology: Part One*, London: Lawrence and Wishart.

Mbembe, Achille (2006) 'Variations on the Beautiful in Congolese Worlds of Sound', in *Beautiful/Ugly: African and Diaspora Aesthetics*, edited by Sarah Nuttall, Durham and London: Duke University Press, pp. 60–93.

McCarthy, Anna (2006) 'From the Ordinary to the Concrete: Cultural Studies and the Politics of Scale', in *Questions of Method in Cultural Studies*, edited by Mimi White and James Schwoch, Oxford: Blackwell, pp. 21–53.

McClintock, Anne (1995) *Imperial Leather: Race, Gender and Sexuality in the Colonial Contest*, London and New York: Routledge.

Macpherson, C. B. (1962) *Political Theory of Possessive Individualism: Hobbes to Locke*, Oxford: Oxford University Press.

Meyer, Erin (2014) *The Culture Map*, New York: Public Affairs.

Miner, Horace (1956) 'Body Ritual among the Nacirema', *American Anthropologist*, Vol. 58, No. 3, pp. 503–7.

Moretti, Franco (2005) *Graphs, Maps, Trees: Abstract Models for a Literary Theory*, London: Verso.

Nash, Roderick (1970) 'The American Invention of National Parks', *American Quarterly*, Vol. 22, No. 3, pp. 726–35.

Orwell, George (1946) 'Why I Write', in *The Collected Essays, Journalism and Letters of George Orwell, Volume 1: An Age Like This 1920–1940*, Harmondsworth: Penguin, 1970, pp. 23–30.

Pauli, Lori (2003) *Manufactured Landscapes: The Photographs of Edward Burtynsky*, New Haven: Yale University Press.

Perec, Georges (2007 [1962]) 'For a Realist Literature', *Chicago Review*, Vol. 54, No. 3–2, pp. 28–39.

Pitt-Rivers, A. H. L-F. (1891) 'Typological museums, as exemplified by the Pitt-Rivers Museum at Oxford, and his Provincial Museum at Farnham, Dorset', *Journal of the Society of Arts*, Vol. 40, December 18, pp. 115–21.

Rabinow, Paul (1977) *Reflections on Fieldwork in Morocco*, Berkeley: University of California Press.

Sedgwick, Eve Kosofsky (2011) *The Weather in Proust*, Durham: Duke University Press.

Sekula, Allan (2002 [1995]) *Fish Story*, Düsseldorf: Richter Verlag.

Seremetakis, C. Nadia (1996) 'The Memory of the Senses, Part 1: Marks of the Transitory' in *The Senses Still: Perception and Memory as Material Culture in Modernity*, edited by Seremetakis, C. Nadia, Chicago: University of Chicago Press, pp. 1–18.

Serres, Michel (1988) 'Turner Translates Carnot', in *Calligram: Essays in New Art History from France*, edited by Norman Bryson, Cambridge: Cambridge University Press, pp. 154–65.

——(1997) 'Science and the Humanities: the Case of Turner', *SubStance*, Vol. 26, No. 2, pp. 6–21.

Shove, Elizabeth (2003) *Comfort, Cleanliness and Convenience: the Social Organization of Normality*, Oxford: Berg.

Smiles, Sam (2000) *J.M.W. Turner*, London: Tate.

Sontag, Susan (1983) *Illness as Metaphor*, London: Penguin.

Stoller, Paul (2004) *Stranger in the Village of the Sick: A Memoir of Cancer, Sorcery, and Healing*, Boston: Beacon Press.

Sweet, Matthew (2014) 'Cheap and Nasty: The Horrid Legacy of the Penny Dreadful', *Guardian*, 6th June, online at: http://www.theguardian.com/books/2014/jun/06/horror-fiction, last accessed 20th January 2015.

Szeman, Imre and Maria Whiteman (2009) 'The Big Picture: On the Politics of Contemporary Photography', *Third Text*, Vol. 23, No. 5, pp. 551–56.

Thompson, E. P. (1961) 'The Long Revolution', *New Left Review*, Vol. 9, pp. 24–33.

——(2013 [1963]) *The Making of the English Working Class*, London: Penguin.

Trumble, William R. and Angus Stevenson (2002) *Shorter Oxford English Dictionary: On Historical Perspectives*, fifth edition, Oxford: Oxford University Press.

Turney, Joanne (2009) *The Culture of Knitting*, London: Bloomsbury.

Tylor, Edward B. (1920 [1871]) *Primitive Culture: Researches into the Development of Mythology, Philosophy, Religion, Language, Art, and Custom*, London: John Murray.

Wainwright, Oliver (2015) 'Mons: it's the European Capital of Culture – but locals just want to go to Ikea', *Guardian Online*, 13th January, http://www.the-guardian.com/artanddesign/2015/jan/13/ last accessed 14th January 2015.

Williams, Raymond (1958) 'Culture is Ordinary', in *Resources of Hope*, London: Verso, 1989, pp. 3–18.

——(1977) *Marxism and Literature*, Oxford: Oxford University Press.

——(1981) *Politics and Letters: Interviews with New Left Review*, London: Verso.

——(1992 [1961]) *The Long Revolution*, London: Hogarth Press.

Williamson, Judith (1986) 'Three Types of Dirt', in *Consuming Passions: The Dynamics of Popular Culture*, London: Marion Boyars, pp. 223–27.

Wilson, Alexander (1992) *The Culture of Nature: North American Landscape from Disney to the Exxon Valdez*, Oxford: Blackwell.

Wittgenstein, Ludwig (1976 [1953]) *Philosophical Investigations*, Oxford: Blackwell.

Woolf, Virginia (2012) *Selected Works of Virginia Woolf*, Ware: Wordsworth Editions.

Wypijewski, Joann, ed. (1999) *Painting by Numbers: Komar and Melamid's Scientific Guide to Art*, Berkeley: University of California Press.

## WEBSITES

DCMS (Department for Culture, Media and Sport) website (2015) https://www.gov.uk/government/organisations/department-for-culture-media-sport, last accessed January 2015.

EU Creative Europe (European Commission) website (2015) http://ec.europa.eu/programmes/creative-europe/actions/capitals-culture_en.htm, last accessed January 2015.

GO-Science (Government Office for Science) website (2015) https://www.gov.uk/government/organisations/government-office-for-science, last accessed January 2015.

*Independent* 21 November 2014 '"Beast of Bolsover" Dennis Skinner takes Ukip MP Mark Reckless to task moments after he is sworn in'

http://www.independent.co.uk/news/uk/politics/labour-mp-dennis-skinner-takes-ukip-mp-mark-reckless-to-task-moments-after-he-is-sworn-in-9875957.html, last accessed February 2015.

National Park Service website 2015, timeline – http://www.nps.gov/parkhistory/hisnps/NPSHistory/timeline_annotated.htm, last accessed January 2015.

Turney, Joanne (2015) Staff Profile – https://applications.bathspa.ac.uk/staff-profiles/profile.asp?user=academic%5Cturj1, last accessed February 2015.

*UK City of Culture 2017: Guidance for Bidding Cities* DCMS (Department for Culture, Media and Sport) website (2015) https://www.gov.uk/government/uploads/system/uploads/attachment_data/file/89369/UK_City_of_Culture_2017_Guidance_and_Criteria.pdf, last accessed January 2015.

## FILMS

*Battleship Potemkin*, directed by Sergei Eisenstein (1925), Mosfilm.

*Leviathan*, directed by Lucien Castaing-Taylor and Verena Paravel (2012), Dogwoof.

*Manufactured Landscapes*, directed by Jennifer Baichwal (2007), BFI.

# INDEX

Abu-Lughod, Lila 78–9
American National Exhibition 73
amyloidosis 120–1
animals 155–7
anthropology 3–4, 28, 31–3, 50–2,
    58–69
Arnold, Matthew 3, 10, 46, 85, 97

Barrell, John 40
Barthes, Roland 28–30
Benedict, Ruth 51–2, 58, 64–5, 100
Benjamin, Walter 83, 86, 88–91, 93
Berger, John 155–6
Berlant, Lauren 147–8
Beveridge, Karl 92–3
*Big Bang Theory, The* (TV
    series) 139
Boas, Franz 52
Book of Leviticus 61–2
Burtynsky, Edward 83–7

*Call of the Wild, The* 26–7
cancer 118, 121, 129–136
Carlson, Jennifer 106–9
Catlin, George 36
Certeau, Michel de 150–1
collective intimacies 145–8
Condé, Carole 92–3
Congolese music 112–14
Connolly, William E. 142–3
Coutts, Marion 131
cultural politics 70–94
cultural reductionism 141–5
culture: dangers of 20–22; definitions
    of 1–5; as distance 16, 101,
    116, 131, 139, 141, 148–51;
    everyday life and 67–9; as

mediation 61–2; as perspective
    13–20, 61, 68, 79, 101–2, 106,
    119, 150
*Culture and Anarchy* 3
*Culture Map, The* 18–19
*Culture of Knitting, The* 14–17
Cvetkovich, Ann 105–6

Darwin, Charles 31
death 117–37
Department for Culture, Media and
    Sport 5–13
diary 120–7
dirt 58–66
Douglas, Mary 60–5, 95

Eliot, T. S. 54–6, 65
Engels, Frederick 29–30, 98
Equality and Human Rights
    Commission 10–11
European Capitals of Culture
    74–5
experience 53–4, 62–4, 74–5, 95–116,
    119–20, 127–8, 131–2, 145–8,
    150–2

Fabian, Johannes 33
feminism 72, 75
*Fighting Téméraire, The* 40–42
Forster, E. M. 138, 140
Frazer, James 50–4

Gallagher, Catherine 143
Gang of Four 115–16
Gawande, Atul 132–5
Geertz, Clifford 66
*Golden Bough, The* 50–4

good life 107–9
Government Office for Science
    (Go-Science) 7–8
Green, Nicholas 34
Greenblatt, Stephen 66–7
Grusin, Richard 37

Haraway, Donna 156
headscarves 77–83

individualism 144–6
intersectionality 144

Keats, John 118–19
Komar and Melamid 34–5

landscape 23–45
Latour, Bruno 141–2
*Leviathan* 87–9
Levine, Caroline 153
literacy 47–8
London, Jack 26
Lubbock, Tom 118–9, 129–131

McCarthy, Anna 148–50
McClintock, Anne 63
Macpherson C. B. 146
Mapplethorpe, Robert 72
Marcus, Greil 114–16
Marx, Karl 29–30
Mbembe, Achille 112–14
Meyer, Erin 18–19
Miner, Horace 59
Muslim women 71, 77–83

National Health Service 120,
    127–8
National Parks 35–38
Natural History Museum 7–8
nature 24–38

ordinary 56, 150–1
Orwell, George 76

patterns 50–8, 64–6, 82–3, 95, 100–1,
    103–4, 111
*Patterns of Culture* 51
Perec, Georges 103–5, 107
Pitt-Rivers, General 31–3
popular culture 47–8
*Primitive Culture* 3
*Purity and Danger* 60–2

Rabinow, Paul 67–8

Science Museum 7–8
Sedgwick, Eve Kosofsky 136–7
Sekula, Allan 89–92
selective tradition 7, 40, 48, 68,
    97–102, 154
Seremetakis, Nadia C. 109–11
Serres, Michel 41–4
Shove, Elizabeth 62–3
Slits, the 114–15
Smiles, Sam 39–40
soap 63–4
Sontag, Susan 118, 127
Stewart, Kathleen 106–9

television 124
things 157–8
Turner, J. M. W. 38–44
Turney, Joanne 14–15
Tylor E. B. 3, 46, 53

UK City of Culture 24–5
UKIP (United Kingdom
    Independence Party) 128

wilderness 24
Williams, Raymond 56–8, 97–8, 100,
    111, 154–5.
Williamson, Judith 64
Wilson, Alexander 24–5
Woolf, Virginia 68
World's Fairs 49–50
Wittgenstein, Ludwig 1

.